D0240188

Turkish

COOKING

Turkish
COOKING

AUTHENTIC CULINARY
TRADITIONS FROM TURKEY

BADE JACKSON

APPLE

A QUINTET BOOK

Published by The Apple Press
6 Blundell Street
London N7 9BH

Copyright © 1998 Quintet Publishing Limited.
All rights reserved. No part of this publication may be reproduced, stored in a retrieval system or transmitted in any form or by any means, electronic, mechanical, photocopying, recording or otherwise, without the permission of the copyright holder.

ISBN 1-85076-994-X

This book was designed and produced by
Quintet Publishing Limited
6 Blundell Street
London N7 9BH

Creative Director: Richard Dewing
Art Director: Clare Reynolds
Designer: Steve West
Project Editor: Diana Steedman
Editor: Rosie Hankin
Food Stylist: Jennie Berresford
Photographer: Andrew Sydenham

Typeset in Great Britain by
Central Southern Typesetters, Eastbourne
Manufactured in Singapore by
Universal Graphics Pte Ltd
Printed in Singapore by
Star Standard Industries Pte Ltd

PICTURE CREDITS

The Publisher would like to thank the following for providing photographs and for permission to reproduce copyright material:

Travel Ink/Abbie Enock: pages 6, 9, 10, 14, 15, 43, 89, 97;
Travel Ink/Luc Janssens: pages 8, 11, 12;
Papilio Photographic: pages 7, 13, 77;
Turkish Information Office, 170-173 Piccadilly, London: pages 27, 67.

Contents

Introduction

Good eating has always played an important role in the long history of the Turks. In Ottoman times they gave as much importance to the building of their kitchens as they did to the building of the palaces they catered for.

Early historical documents show that the basic structure of Turkish cuisine was already established during the nomadic period of the sixth to eleventh century AD, and in the first settled Turkish states of Asia, which were peopled by descendants of the tribes who fought with the Mongols in the thirteenth century. Culinary attitudes towards meat, dairy products, vegetables and grains that characterised this period still make up the core of Turkish cuisine. The importance of the culinary art for the Ottoman sultans is evident to every visitor to Topkapi Palace. The huge kitchens were housed in several buildings under ten domes. By the seventeenth century, some thirteen hundred kitchen staff were housed in the palace.

Hundreds of cooks, specialising in different categories of dishes, such as soups, pilafs, kebabs, helva, beverages, and so on, fed as many as ten thousand people a day and, in addition, sent trays of food to others in the city as a royal favour. It was in this environment that hundreds of the Sultan's chefs, who dedicated their lives to their profession, developed and perfected the dishes of Turkish cuisine, which was then adopted by the kitchens of the provinces ranging from the Balkans to southern Russia, and down to North Africa. The spice route, the most important factor in culinary history, was under the full control of the Sultan and only the best ingredients were allowed to be traded under the strict standards established by the courts.

Left: **For centuries the Topkapi Palace provided a rich backdrop to the feasting of the Ottoman sultans. Underneath the sumptuous courtyards lay the legendary kitchens, built in 1453, where thousands of chefs aimed for culinary perfection.**

Above: **The famous bazaars are riots of colour where huge quantities of produce change hands at furious pace. Here, locals hunt for bargains at the Calatasary Fish Market.**

A cuisine of delicacy and richness

Turkey, with its long history of ancient civilisations, its fertile lands and geographical setting between Asia and Europe, stretches a thousand miles from east to west, and covers an area equal to half the size of Mexico. It follows therefore that the cuisine of this country is diverse. The choice of dishes is wide, but all have a wonderful delicacy and richness.

Istanbul is well known for the richness and diversity of its cuisine as well as for its lavish entertainments. A fantastic variety of fresh fish from the Marmara Sea

and Black Sea, local high-quality vineyards and an abundance of fresh produce as varied as olives, figs, fruit and vegetables, combining with citizens from every corner of Turkey and beyond, make the list of recipes seem endless.

Turkey's Black Sea region, where the Anatolian plateau falls through vast forests of pine, fruit, and nut trees to a sea famous for its lobsters, caviar and anchovies, is justly proud of its reputation for pasta and seafood dishes. Pasta or *makarna* is produced locally in a wide variety of forms, and contributes to many delicious specialities.

Eastern Turkey, bordering Georgia, Syria, Iran and Iraq, with its high mountains, plains and its ethnic mix, serves a variety of hot and spicy dishes. Using locally grown pistachios and exotic fruits, the eastern region is also famous for its desserts, such as widely known baklava and the local sherbets.

***Above*: Fresh vegetables, such as these cucumbers, are bought on a daily basis from traders for use in salads, *kebabs* and *dolmas*.**

There are several types of sherbets made in Turkey. The traditonal varieties are still drinks that are made for special occasions such as the birth of a baby. They are made of sherbet candy which consists of traditonally dried and pressed fruits and flowers.

The southern region, with its lacelike coastline, contributes with mouthwatering Mediterranean dishes. Here there is an abundance of seafood, and a dazzling choice of local produce including fruits, nuts, olives and vines.

Even at the centre of Turkey, in the capital city of Ankara, surrounded by mountains, you can still buy an impressive variety of fresh fish, vegetables, and fruit daily. This is very important to the cook, as the use of frozen food is minimal, and the range of menus extensive. As each region has its specialities, so does each town, and each individual has his or her favourite dishes, but it is fair to say that the traditional Turkish household uses many of the recipes included in this book.

Turkish serving traditions

Turkish cooking takes time, effort and organisation. In Turkey food is bought fresh daily, and each meal of the day would be taken into account, with as much attention paid to breakfast as to lunch, supper, or dinner. As well as having a balance of nutrients, food should also be appealing to the eye, and, of course, tasty. Turkey, with its vast forests, fertile seas and abundant lands, produces all the food to meet the country's needs. Her people are self-sufficient in all produce and

appreciate the natural goodness of organic food. Turkish cuisine is healthy and nutritious and the Turks are purist in their culinary taste; their dishes bring out the flavour of the main ingredient rather than hiding it behind sauces or spices, therefore spices and herbs are used very sparingly and singly.

Turkish people by nature like to be at the dinner table as long as possible, to enjoy their food to the maximum, to relax while eating it, and to converse over it. Appetisers form an important part of the cuisine. The kitchens of Topkapi Palace in Istanbul, dating from the Conqueror Fatih (1453), were decorated and fitted out in a manner worthy of their imperial function. The huge cauldron, the two great casseroles, together capable of containing several tons of food, and the gigantic soup ladles, which are all on display in their original places, are sufficient to point to the importance of soups in Turkish cuisine. It was in the same place that the janissaries, the élite soldiers of the Sultan's armies, received their thrice-yearly pay and swallowed down their legendary soup, as well as distributing palace *baklava* on feast days to the less fortunate.

***Below:* Galata Bridge, spanning Istanbul's Golden Horn, is always filled with a dazzling array of hawkers, selling anything from sweet sherbet to roasted corn-on-the-cob.**

Right: The breathtaking interior of the Aya Sofya museum. From the outside, this dome dominates the skyline of old Istanbul.

Appetisers

The tradition of serving four hot and four cold appetisers, preferably including a soup, is still very much alive in Turkey today. In the capital city of Ankara, all the restaurants still offer you a trolley full of cold and hot appetisers to choose from, before your main course is even ordered. During Ramadan, when Muslims fast throughout the day, only to eat in the evening at *iftar,* with all the Muslims in the world, the *iftar* tables would carry a menu of appetisers. Cheese, spinach, and meat boreks, soups, salads, rose petal and fig jams, cold dolmas and, of course, olives to start, symbolise peace.

Above: Turkish rugs hang from the walls of the covered market (Kapali Carsi).

Turkish people are fond of cold appetisers that contain olive oil. We call them *zeytinyagli yemekler*: 'olive oil dishes'. The traditional Turkish family would think little of your cooking if you did not serve at least two hot and two cold appetisers, with a salad.

Cooking with olive oil is also a good way of preserving vegetables. They will keep, covered, in the fridge for a few days, although it is recommended that any recipes with a flavouring such as garlic added to the olive oil should not be kept more than 12 hours, as there can be a danger of botulism after this time. It is also recommended that a high-quality olive oil is used, a good indication of this being the price paid for the oil.

You do not have to go as far as the pastry houses or restaurants to be offered a choice of appetisers in modern Turkey. Even travelling by train, you can still expect to be served with delicious *sigara borek,* cold dolmas and salads, before ordering your main course.

Kebabs and Dolmas

Kebap is another category of food which is typically Turkish, dating back to the times when the nomadic Turks learned to grill and roast their meat over the campfires. Given the numerous types of kebaps, it helps to realise that you categorise them by the way the meat is cooked, as in *sis kebap* and *doner kebap.* It is not that they are complicated or even particularly exotic, but their basic flavour and combination of simple ingredients has stood the test of time. The preparation of doner kebap always follows the traditional methods. First the boned leg of lamb is marinated with herbs, yogurt, tomato and onions for a few hours, then it is sliced thinly, and wrapped around a vertical spit and placed in front of a three-tiered upright grill. As the spit revolves slowly, the outside layer of the lamb cooks. From this revolving action the dish takes its name *doner,* which means 'to turn' in Turkish. Sis kebap is another way of cooking meat. *Sis* means

عثمان
رضي الله عنه

skewer in Turkish. In Nomadic times the meat was cooked slowly over the camp fires along with onions, peppers and herbs. It should be noted that the unique taste of kebaps is due more to the breeds of sheep and cattle which are raised in open pastures, than to their special marinades and the way of cooking.

Dolma is the generic term for stuffed vegetables; being a derivative of the verb *doldurmak*, meaning 'to fill', it actually means 'stuffed' in Turkish. There are two types of dolma: those filled with a minced meat mix and those filled with a rice mix. The latter are cooked in olive oil and eaten at room temperature. The meat dolma is a main course dish, eaten with a yoghurt sauce, and is frequently prepared in an average household.

Left: **Colourful cherry-juice sellers clad in tarbooshes offer round-the-clock refreshment for thirsty diners.**

Desserts and Drinks

The most common dessert served is seasonal fruits that acquire their unique taste from the abundance of sun and the traditional methods of cultivation. For most of the spring and summer, fruit is eaten fresh. Later on into the autumn, the fruit may be used dried, in compotes, or made into preserves. Among the special preserves are marmalades, made from quince or sour cherries, and those prepared using figs or delicate rose petals.

There is not a spot with a view, or a park in Turkey without its tea or coffee house. A great deal has been written about Turkish coffee, its history, its significance in social life and the ambience of the coffee houses, and yet the tiny brew with its annoying grounds can be a disappointment to the uninitiated. A few words of caution—the grounds are not to be swallowed! Secondly, do not expect a caffeine surge—it is not strong coffee, just thick. And, remember, it is actually the setting and the company that matter: the coffee is just an excuse for an occasion to socialise.

Above: **The panels of the Sultan's Harem in Topkapi Palace are stunning displays of Turkish handcraftman's skills.**

Other beverages that are distinctly Turkish are *Boza,* a thick, fermented drink made from wheat berries; *Sahlep,* a hot drink made with powdered roots of certain orchids; *Ayran,* a refreshing drink made with yoghurt; and the many excellent bottled pure fruit juices.

Afiyet Olsun

In the following recipes, I have tried to include a wide variety of meat and vegetable dishes—many that would be prepared in an average Turkish household, and other more unusual recipes—all with easily available ingredients. All the dishes in this book are tried and tested. In most cases you will have no difficulty obtaining all the ingredients, and where there is any doubt you will find alternative suggestions. I hope you will enjoy the dishes as much as we do, and, as we say in Turkey, *Afiyet Olsun*, which means 'good appetite'.

Fade J Jackson

Soups and Salads

CORBALAR VE SALATALAR

Yoghurt Soup

YOGURT CORBASI

This is the kind of soup that you can serve to someone who is feeling a little 'under the weather'. It is still called in some regions hasta corbasi *which means 'soup for the ill'. The ingredients differ slightly from region to region, but I prefer this version which is a cross between yoghurt and yayla soup. Yayla soup can be literally translated as 'soup from the valley' and is exactly the same as Yoghurt Soup with the addition, while simmering, of a chopped tomato.*

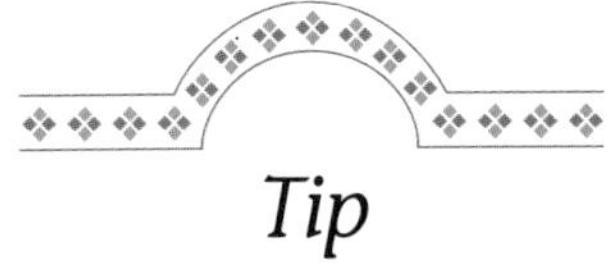

Tip

Turkish yoghurts are thick and creamy and very similar to Greek yoghurt. In all the recipes calling for yoghurt, use a thick, unsweetened set yoghurt.

Serves 4

15 g/½ oz butter or margarine
1 Tbsp flour
250 ml/9 fl oz plain yoghurt, strained
1 l/1¾ pts chicken stock
1 Tbsp rice, washed and drained (optional)
Salt and ground black pepper
Dried mint and paprika, to garnish
Croûtons, to serve

PREPARATION TIME: **5 MINUTES**
COOKING TIME: **25 MINUTES**

1. Heat the butter or margarine in a large saucepan and add the flour. Stirring continuously, brown gently over medium heat until smooth.

2. Mix in the yoghurt, and stir thoroughly, then slowly add the chicken stock.

3. Bring to the boil and add the rice, if using. Season well, cover, and simmer gently for about 15 minutes, or until the rice is soft. Garnish with dried mint and paprika, and serve hot with croûtons.

Ezo Bride Soup

EZO GELIN CORBASI

This soup has its origins in an ancient folkloric tale. According to the story the soup was cooked in celebration of the wedding of Ezo, a chieftain's beautiful daughter, who was married near a famous bridge over the river Kizil Irmak. The story has an unhappy ending, so I will not disclose it, to avoid putting you off this fine soup.

Serves 4

50 g/2 oz butter plus a little extra
1 small onion, chopped
1 l/1¾ pts chicken stock
100 g/4 oz fine bulgur, cracked wheat
100 g/4 oz red lentils
1 Tbsp tomato purée
Salt and ground black pepper
2 tsp paprika

PREPARATION TIME: **10 MINUTES**
COOKING TIME: **30 MINUTES**

1. Heat the 50 g/2 oz butter in a saucepan and fry the onion. Pour in the chicken stock and bring steadily to the boil.

2. Add the bulgur wheat, red lentils and tomato purée. Stir, then simmer for 20 minutes over low heat. Taste and adjust the seasoning if necessary.

3. Just before serving, melt a knob of butter in a frying pan, stir in the paprika, and then pour over the soup.

Wedding Soup

DUGUN CORBASI

This is a delicious soup that is traditionally served at weddings. However, it is not necessary to wait for a wedding among your family or friends to enjoy it!

Serves 4

250 g/9 oz finely diced mutton
1 onion, peeled and left whole
1 carrot, peeled and left whole
1 l/1¾ pts water
30 g/1 oz butter
1 Tbsp flour
2 small eggs
Juice of 1 lemon
1 tsp paprika or chilli powder
Salt and ground black pepper

PREPARATION TIME: **10 MINUTES**
COOKING TIME: **35 MINUTES**

1. Place the meat, onion and carrot in a saucepan with the water, cover, and bring to the boil. Simmer gently for 1 hour. Discard the onion and carrot.

2. Melt half the butter in another pan, add the flour, and brown lightly. Slowly pour in the prepared stock and bring to the boil. Cover and simmer for 20 minutes until the meat is tender.

3. Break the eggs into a bowl, add the lemon juice, and beat well. Carry on beating the mixture while adding, little by little, a tablespoon of the soup. Pour the mixture into the soup, stirring continuously. Turn off the heat.

4. Melt the remaining butter in a small frying pan, stir in the paprika or chilli powder, then pour over the soup. Season well and serve.

Tip

If you cannot find mutton, substitute lamb. The dish will not be so full flavoured but it will still be delicious.

Behind every good soup, stew or sauce is a well-made stock. Stock cubes, while convenient, are usually over salty. Homemade stocks are simple to make, and enhance your recipes beyond measure. As for fish and vegetables—you can vary the ingredients according to your taste. It is just a matter of placing the ingredients in a saucepan of cold water and simmering gently for 1 to 2 hours. Store your supply in the freezer in varying quantities, ready to hand.

Chicken Stock

PREPARATION TIME: **5 MINUTES**
COOKING TIME: **1 HOUR MINIMUM**

a chicken carcass
2 leeks, white parts only, washed
1 large onion, peeled and quartered
2 carrots, washed
several sprigs of parsley
3 celery stalks
6 black peppercorns
3½ l/6 pts water

1 Place all the ingredients in a large pan. Pour in the water, cover, and slowly bring to the boil. Skim off the fat and foam.
2 Simmer, covered, for at least 1 hour. Strain, cool and store either in the refrigerator or in the freezer.

Meat Stock

PREPARATION TIME: **10 MINUTES**
COOKING TIME: **2 HOURS MINIMUM**

450 g/1 lb beef pieces, coarsely chopped
2 leeks, white parts only, washed
1 large onion, peeled and halved
2 carrots, washed
several sprigs of parsley
1 garlic clove
3½ l/6 pts water
6 black peppercorns

1 Place all the vegetables and meat in a large pan, pour in the water and slowly bring to the boil. Skim off the fat and foam. Add the black peppercorns, and simmer, covered, for at least 2 hours, topping up with a little water as necessary and skimming occasionally.
2 Strain, cool and store either in the refrigerator or in the freezer.

Chicken and Noodle Soup

SEHRIYE CORBASI

This soup is very popular with children and is a good way of introducing them to soup. The crafty addition of star-shaped noodles, or something similar, will entice them to try at least just a spoonful.

Serves 4

30 g/1 oz butter
150 g/5 oz chicken, chopped fine
2 fresh ripe tomatoes, chopped
825 ml/1½ pts chicken stock
1 carrot, diced
60 g/2 oz noodles
Salt and ground black pepper
Juice of ½ lemon
Chopped fresh parsley, to garnish

PREPARATION TIME: **5 MINUTES**
COOKING TIME: **25 MINUTES**

1. Melt the butter in a saucepan and fry the chicken for 1 minute.

2. Add the tomatoes, stir, and pour in the chicken stock. Bring to the boil, then add the carrot and noodles. Cover and simmer for 20 minutes.

3. Just before serving, season well and add the lemon juice. Serve hot, garnished with chopped parsley.

Lentil Soup

MERCIMEK CORBASI

This is one of my favourite winter soups, and it is both nourishing and satisfying. The addition of cumin is an Anatolian variation that gives a distinctive taste.

Serves 4

15 g/½ oz butter or margarine
1 small onion, chopped
1 carrot, diced
825 ml/1½ pts chicken stock
200 g/7 oz green lentils
1 tsp ground cumin
Salt and ground black pepper
Chopped fresh parsley, to garnish (optional)

PREPARATION TIME: **5 MINUTES**
COOKING TIME: **25 MINUTES**

1. Heat the butter and fry the onion until soft. Add the carrot and cook for 1 minute.

2. Pour in the chicken stock and add the lentils. Bring to the boil over medium heat and stir in the cumin. Simmer for 20 minutes. Pass soup through a metal sieve, or purée in a blender or food processor.

3. Return to the pan, reheat, taste and adjust the seasoning, and serve with parsley scattered over, if using.

Green Salad

YESIL SALATA

This is a very basic salad, but nevertheless often used in Turkish cooking especially with grilled meats. The basis of the salad is green lettuce, hence the given name, but it is usually made as follows.

Serves 4

225 g/8 oz mixed salad leaves
2 spring onions, chopped
2 fresh tomatoes, sliced
3 radishes, sliced
2 hard-boiled eggs
2 Tbsp each chopped fresh dill and parsley
3 or 4 black olives, pitted and chopped
1½ Tbsp olive oil
1½ Tbsp lemon juice
Salt and ground black pepper
Feta cheese cubes, to garnish

PREPARATION TIME: **15 MINUTES**

1. Wash the salad leaves, dry in a salad spinner or clean tea towel, and put into a large salad bowl. Arrange the spring onions, sliced tomatoes, and radishes over the salad leaves.

2. Cut the eggs into wedges lengthwise. Add to the salad bowl, along with the dill, parsley, and olives.

3. To make the dressing, combine the olive oil, lemon juice, and seasoning to taste. Then pour over the salad. Garnish with small cubes of feta cheese before serving.

Bean Salad

PIYAZ

In most Turkish streets you can find a kofte *restaurant where this salad would be most popular. Use any type of white bean you like in this dish, although broad beans will disintegrate a bit. Check the package for cooking times.*

Serves 4

200 g/7 oz haricot beans
2 tomatoes, chopped
1 green pepper or chilli, chopped
1 onion, chopped
A handful of fresh parsley, chopped
Salt and ground black pepper
2 hard-boiled eggs
3 radishes, sliced
1 Tbsp red wine vinegar
1 Tbsp olive oil
4 black olives, to garnish

PREPARATION TIME: **OVERNIGHT PLUS 20 MINUTES**

1. Soak the beans overnight, drain, and place in a saucepan with plenty of water. Bring to the boil and simmer until tender. Drain, rinse in cold water, and drain again. Place in a serving dish and add the tomatoes and green pepper or chilli.

2. In a separate bowl rub the onion with a little salt, then wash, and drain. Add the onion to the salad, along with the parsley, and season to taste.

3. Cut the eggs lengthwise into wedges. Arrange the eggs and the radishes over the salad.

4. Mix the vinegar with the olive oil, and pour over the salad. Garnish with olives and serve.

Aubergine Salad with Yoghurt

YOGURTLU PATLICAN SALATA

This salad is very well known in Turkey as it is usually served with the potent Turkish spirit, Raki. *It is served everywhere from a seaside bar to a five-star hotel.*

Serves 4

- 2 aubergines
- 150 g/6 oz plain yoghurt
- 2 garlic cloves, crushed
- 1 green pepper, seeded, grilled until soft, and chopped
- 1 large fresh tomato, peeled and chopped
- 1 Tbsp olive oil
- Juice of 1 lemon
- Salt and ground black pepper
- A few black olives

PREPARATION TIME: **40 MINUTES**

1. Prepare the aubergines in the same way as for Aubergine Salad (see page 24). Once peeled, mash the flesh, and place in a salad bowl.
2. Stir in the yoghurt, garlic, green pepper and tomato.
3. Combine the olive oil and lemon juice to make the dressing, adding seasoning to taste. Pour over the salad and garnish with a few olives.

Houmous

HUMUS

This is the traditional Turkish version of the well-known salad, and is quite a different taste than a shop-bought one. If you cannot find tahini (ground sesame seeds) in your supermarket, try a speciality shop or a delicatessen.

Serves 4

- 250 g/9 oz chick peas
- 100 ml/4 fl. oz tahini
- 1 garlic clove, crushed
- 2 Tbsp lemon juice
- 1 Tbsp olive oil
- ½ tsp paprika
- Salt and ground black pepper
- Crackers or toasted bread, to serve

PREPARATION TIME: **OVERNIGHT PLUS 2 HOURS**

1. Soak the chick peas overnight, drain well, and put in a saucepan with plenty of water to cover. Bring to the boil and simmer until soft, about 2½ hours. (Skinned chick peas will cook in about 1½ hours.)
2. Remove the skins from the chick peas and mash until smooth, adding a little water if necessary.
3. Add the rest of the ingredients, and season to taste. Mix well and place in a serving dish. Serve with crackers or toasted bread.

Bulgur Wheat Salad

KISIR

This is a very nutritious and filling salad. It is probably a good idea, therefore, to serve it with a light meal, such as simply grilled meat.

Serves 4

250 g/9 oz bulgur wheat
1 Tbsp tomato purée
4 spring onions, trimmed and chopped
A handful of fresh mint, chopped
A handful of fresh parsley, chopped
Juice of 1 lemon
Salt and ground black pepper
2 cos lettuce leaves, torn

PREPARATION TIME: **20 MINUTES**

1. Place the bulgur wheat in a bowl and cover with boiling water. Soak for 5 minutes, or until the water is absorbed.

2. Stir in the tomato purée. When thoroughly mixed, add the spring onions and herbs.

3. Pour over the lemon juice, taste, and season with salt and pepper. Serve garnished with the torn lettuce leaves.

Aubergine Salad

PATLICAN SALATA

This is one of my favourite salads. It is traditionally cooked over an open fire to accompany grilled meats. You can prepare it using the gas hob if you don't mind the mess.

Serves 4

1 aubergine
1 large fresh tomato, peeled and chopped
1 green pepper, finely sliced
1 large garlic clove, crushed
1 onion, chopped
Salt and ground black pepper
A handful of fresh parsley, chopped
Juice of 1 lemon
1 Tbsp olive oil

PREPARATION TIME: **40 MINUTES**

1. Wash the aubergine and prick all over with a fork. Place on the barbecue (before the meat as it takes longer to cook). To make sure it cooks evenly, turn it occasionally using the stem as a handle. When the skin of the aubergine looks quite burnt, make sure the flesh is soft right through by testing it with a fork.

2. Hold the aubergine under cold running water to cool, then peel the skin, leaving the soft flesh. Slice it into a serving dish and add the tomatoes, green pepper and garlic.

3. Place the onion in a separate dish and rub with a good pinch of salt, then wash and drain. Add to the salad along with the parsley.

4. To make the dressing, combine the lemon juice, olive oil, and salt and pepper to taste. Drizzle over the salad and serve.

Tip

When raw onion appears in a recipe, chop or slice it as required, then rub a little salt into it. Then wash and drain before adding to the dish. This softens the onion slightly, making it much more palatable.

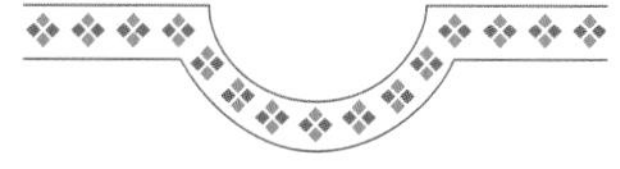

Yoghurt Hors d'Oeuvres

CACIK

This dish is often served with four or five other appetisers at the beginning of any meal, and while it is used as a dip in some countries, in Turkey it is served in individual bowls and eaten with a spoon.

Serves 4

- 450 g/15 oz plain yoghurt
- 2 garlic cloves, crushed
- 1 small or a ½ large cucumber
- 1 Tbsp dried mint
- 1 Tbsp dried dill
- 1 tsp olive oil
- A few fresh mint leaves and ice cubes, to garnish

PREPARATION TIME: **10 MINUTES**

1. Place the yoghurt in a bowl and add the garlic.

2. Peel the cucumber and dice finely. Stir into the yoghurt with the dried herbs. Mix well and add a little water if the *cacik* is too thick.

3. Sprinkle with the olive oil and serve, garnished with mint leaves and ice cubes.

Shepherd's Salad

COBAN SALATA

This salad owes its origins to the meal that a shepherd would take for his mid-day meal. The simple ingredients of onion, tomato, cucumber and green pepper would be garnished with herbs that he might gather from the mountainside. My recipe is a formalised version enjoyed in the city.

Serves 4

1 onion
Salt and ground black pepper
2 large fresh tomatoes
1 small cucumber
1 green pepper, seeded and diced
1 chilli, finely diced (optional)
A handful of fresh parsley, chopped
A handful of fresh dill (optional)
1 Tbsp olive oil
1 Tbsp lemon juice
A few black olives, to garnish

PREPARATION TIME: **15 MINUTES**

1. Slice the onion into thin half circles. Place in a bowl and rub with a little salt, then wash, and drain.

2. Chop the tomatoes and place in a serving dish with the onions.

3. Peel the cucumber, dice, and add to the bowl.

4. Stir in the green pepper, chilli, if using, and the herbs.

5. Drizzle the salad with the olive oil and lemon juice, season to taste, and serve garnished with olives.

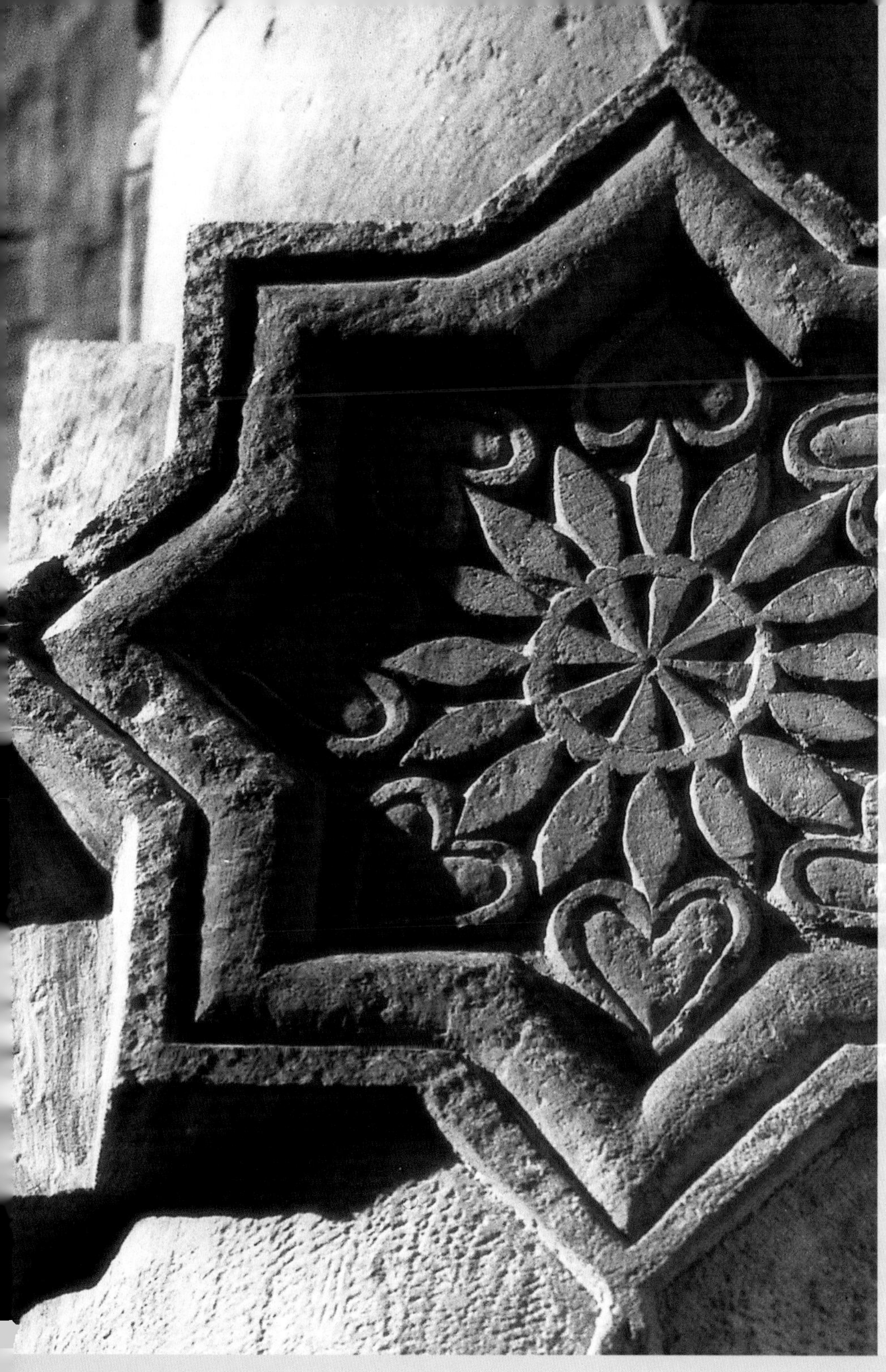

Cold and Hot Appetisers

BASLANGICLAR
SOGUK MEZELER
VE SICAK MEZELER

French Beans Cooked in Olive Oil

ZEYTINYAGLI FASULYE

This is a very common olive oil appetiser to be served with almost any meat dish.

Serves 4

100 ml/¼ pt olive oil
1 onion, chopped
500 g/1 lb French beans, trimmed
1 large fresh tomato, skinned and chopped
1 Tbsp tomato purée
Salt and ground black pepper
Chopped fresh parsley, to garnish

PREPARATION TIME: **15 MINUTES**
COOKING TIME: **30 MINUTES**

1. Heat the oil in a frying pan and fry the onions until transparent, then add the beans, and fry together for a few minutes.

2. Cover with cold water, then add the chopped tomato. Bring to the boil and stir in the tomato purée, then reduce the heat, and simmer for 20 minutes, or until the beans are cooked. Drain, retaining about 1 tablespoon of the cooking juice.

3. Transfer the beans to a glass dish and add the retained juice. Season to taste. Chill before serving, garnished with parsley.

Beans Cooked in Olive Oil

BAKLA

This is a very nutritious dish, and the brightness of the beans is much improved by the addition of the dill, especially if it is fresh.

Serves 4

100 ml/¼ pt olive oil
1 kg/2 lb fresh broad beans
1 large onion, cut into rings
1 Tbsp chopped fresh dill
1 Tbsp sugar
Juice of 1 lemon
Salt and ground black pepper
1 Tbsp chopped fresh parsley
Plain yoghurt, to serve

PREPARATION TIME: **20 MINUTES**
COOKING TIME: **1 HOUR 10 MINUTES**

1. Heat the oil in a saucepan, stir in the beans, and fry for a few minutes.

2. Line another saucepan with half the onion rings and place the beans evenly on top. Layer the remaining onions on top of the beans and add the dill, sugar, lemon juice, seasoning, and 350 ml/12 fl. oz water. Cover with greaseproof paper and cook for about 1 hour, or until tender. If the beans are tinned they will require less cooking time. Remove from heat and allow to cool.

3. Transfer to a serving dish and scatter parsley over. Serve with plain yoghurt.

Leeks Cooked in Olive Oil

ZEYTINYAGLI PIRASA

Although this sounds a rather humble dish, it is quite popular and is surprisingly refreshing with the combination of freshly squeezed lemon juice, leeks and carrots cooked in extra virgin olive oil.

Serves 4

100 ml/¼ pt olive oil
1 onion, chopped
500 g/1 lb leeks, chopped
1 carrot, sliced
100 g/4 oz long grain rice, washed and drained
1 tomato, skinned and chopped
1 tsp sugar
Salt and ground black pepper
Juice of ½ lemon
Lemon wedges, to serve

PREPARATION TIME: **15 MINUTES**
COOKING TIME: **25 MINUTES**

1. Heat the oil in a saucepan and fry the onion until soft. Then add the leeks, carrots and rice, and fry together for a few minutes, stirring occasionally.

2. Add water to cover and bring to the boil over medium heat. Add the tomato, sugar and seasoning to taste, then reduce the heat, and simmer, covered, for 20 minutes, until the water is reduced by half and the rice is cooked.

3. Allow to cool, then place in a serving dish. Sprinkle with the lemon juice and serve with lemon wedges for squeezing over.

Fava Bean Mould

FAVA

Fava beans might be difficult to obtain from a supermarket. They are sometimes known as dried broad beans. You may be able to get them from a delicatessen or, if not, then any dried beans will do. The finished dish might not be as firm as it is supposed to be, but it will taste just as good.

Serves 4

500 g/1 lb fava beans
250 ml/½ pt olive oil, plus extra to glaze
1 onion, quartered
1 tsp sugar
Juice of 1 lemon
Salt and ground black pepper
Chopped fresh parsley, to garnish

PREPARATION TIME:
OVERNIGHT PLUS 10 MINUTES
COOKING TIME:
45 MINUTES PLUS CHILLING TIME

1. Soak the beans overnight.

2. Heat the oil in a saucepan and fry the onion for a few minutes. Add 400 ml/1 pt water, or just enough water to cover the onions, and bring to the boil.

3. Drain the beans and add to the onions. Simmer for 10 minutes then add the sugar, lemon juice and seasoning. Simmer the mixture for 30 minutes more, or until the beans are tender.

4. Purée the beans with a little of the cooking water by pressing them through a metal sieve with a wooden spoon, or use a blender or food processor, and place in an oiled 18-cm/7-inch ring mould.

5. Chill for 2 hours. When chilled, place a serving plate over the mould, invert, and turn out the purée. Brush with a little olive oil and garnish with parsley.

Tip

Cooking dried beans and peas in a pressure cooker reduces the cooking time dramatically. Always refer to the instructions on the package.

Aubergine Cooked in Olive Oil

PATLICAN IMAM BAYILDI

Aubergine is a special favourite in Turkey. There are said to be over a hundred ways of cooking it! Many of these have picturesque names, like imam bayildi, *translated as the 'Imam fainted', presumably from delight at such a delicious dish, or maybe the description of the striped aubergine resembles the Imam lying down in his traditional clothes.*

Serves 3

3 aubergines
200 ml/½ pt olive oil
1 onion, chopped
2 large, fresh ripe tomatoes, skinned and chopped
1 garlic clove, crushed
Juice of ½ lemon
1 tsp sugar
Salt and ground black pepper
3 firm, fresh tomatoes, sliced
Chopped fresh parsley, to garnish

PREPARATION TIME: **20 MINUTES**
COOKING TIME: **45 MINUTES**

1. Peel the aubergine skin in stripes lengthwise. Cut a slit in the aubergines and scoop out most of the flesh, being careful not to pierce the skin. Discard the flesh.

2. Heat 1 tablespoon of the olive oil in a heatproof casserole and fry the aubergines for a few minutes, until nicely coloured.

3. Pour the remaining oil into a saucepan, and fry the onions until soft. Stir in the chopped tomatoes and garlic, and fry together for a few minutes.

4. Drain the aubergines, fill with the vegetable mixture, then return to the casserole, slit side up, with enough water to cover. Stir in the lemon juice, sugar, and salt and pepper to taste. Cover and simmer for about 15 minutes over medium heat.

5. Place a sliced tomato on each aubergine and simmer for 10 minutes more over low heat, until the aubergines are soft but retain their shape. Allow to cool, then place in a serving dish, and garnish with parsley.

Circassian Chicken

CERKEZ TAVUGU

Circassia, situated on the Black Sea on the north of the Caucasus mountains, was a region famous in the times of the Ottoman Empire for its horses, horsemen and horsewomen. The game of 'Cirit', similar to polo, was imported to Istanbul along with this famous recipe.

Serves 6

1 small fresh chicken
1 onion, sliced
Salt and ground black pepper
500 g/1 lb walnuts, shelled and peeled
350 g/12 oz fresh breadcrumbs
1 tsp chilli powder or paprika
Olive oil, to glaze
Chopped hot chilli, to garnish

PREPARATION TIME: **20 MINUTES**
COOKING TIME: **60 MINUTES**

1. Wash the chicken and place it in a large saucepan with the onion. Pour enough water to cover and bring to the boil. Simmer for about 40 minutes, depending on the size of the chicken, until well cooked.

2. When cooked, reserve the stock, and skin and bone the chicken. Chop the meat into very small pieces and place in a serving dish. Season with salt and pepper.

3. Put the walnuts in a blender or food processor and finely chop. Then add half the breadcrumbs and half the chilli powder or paprika. Blend for 1 minute, then add the rest of the breadcrumbs and spice, and blend thoroughly.

4. Place the mixture in a mixing bowl and stir in some of the reserved chicken stock until it reaches the consistency of double cream.

5. Place half the chicken pieces in the serving dish, cover with the sauce and sprinkle the remaining chicken pieces over the top. Brush with a little olive oil and sprinkle with chopped fresh chilli.

Tip

To peel walnuts, soak them in boiling water and leave until the water cools down. The peel will come away easily, but it is important to carry out the task as soon as they are cool enough to handle, otherwise a bitter flavour is imparted to the nut.

Potatoes With Cheese

PEYNIRLI PATATES

This is a very light dish and can be served as a snack or as a side dish.

Serves 4

500 g/1 lb mashed potato
100 g/4 oz grated Cheddar cheese
100 g/4 oz butter
Salt and ground black pepper
3 eggs

PREPARATION TIME: **20 MINUTES**
COOKING TIME: **25 MINUTES**

1. Preheat oven to 200ºC/400ºF/ Gas Mark 6. Place the mashed potato with the cheese, butter and seasoning in a large bowl and mix thoroughly, gradually folding in two of the eggs.

2. Shape the mixture into a cylinder and cut into circles. Place on a greased baking tray and brush with egg yolk. Cook for about 20 minutes, until golden. Serve hot.

Albanian Liver

ARNAVUT CIGERI

Make sure you use lamb's liver for this dish. Ox liver can be substituted but it requires long, slow cooking and is therefore not so suitable.

Serves 4

Olive oil, for shallow frying
2 Tbsp flour
Salt and ground black pepper
250 g/9 oz lamb's liver, diced
1 bunch spring onions, chopped
2 Tbsp chopped fresh parsley

PREPARATION TIME: **15 MINUTES**
COOKING TIME: **25 MINUTES**

1. Heat the oil in a large frying pan. Place the flour in a bowl and stir in some seasoning. Dip each piece of liver in the flour, shake off the excess, and fry in the pan. Turn occasionally for even colouring. Do not overcook as this would harden and dry the liver.

2. Drain, place in a warm serving dish, and garnish with spring onions and parsley. Serve immediately.

Cigarette Pies

SIGARA BOREGI

This is one of my favourite appetisers and it can be rolled in advance. Simply sprinkle the pies with flour to prevent sticking, cover, and keep in the refrigerator for later use.

Serves 4

250 g/8 oz filo pastry, fresh or frozen
Olive oil, for shallow frying

FOR THE FILLING
250 g/8 oz mashed potato
1 onion, finely chopped
60 g/2 oz Cheddar cheese, grated
2 Tbsp chopped fresh parsley
Pinch of paprika
Salt and ground black pepper

PREPARATION TIME: **30 MINUTES**
COOKING TIME: **30 MINUTES**

Tip

You can make this borek using different fillings, too. Try feta cheese with some chopped fresh parsley and seasoning or a filling of minced beef or lamb cooked with some chopped onion.

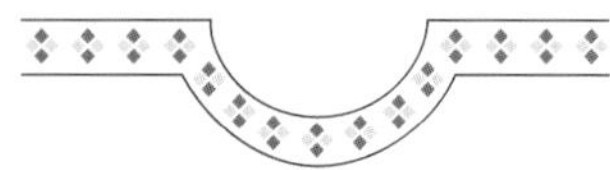

1. On a floured board, cut filo pastry into 7.5-cm/3-inch triangles. Keep them under a damp tea towel to prevent them from becoming brittle.

2. Mix all the filling ingredients together in a bowl and season well. Place 1 teaspoon of the stuffing at the centre of one side of the triangle, fold the two corners over the stuffing, then roll like a cigarette, sealing the edge with a little water. Repeat with all the remaining pastry sheets.

3. Heat the oil in a frying pan and fry the boreks on all sides until golden. Place in a serving dish lined with kitchen paper, to absorb the excess oil, and serve while still hot.

Fried Vegetables

KIZARTMA

This is a very colourful dish and can be made in advance and kept in the refrigerator for a few hours. It is just as good cold or hot. You can use a variety of vegetables for different tastes.

Serves 4

Olive oil, for shallow frying
1 aubergine, peeled and sliced into rings
1 large potato, peeled and sliced
2 green or red peppers, pricked
2 chillis, pricked
1 courgette, sliced
Flour, for coating
3 fresh ripe tomatoes, chopped
1 Tbsp chopped parsley
1 garlic clove, crushed
Plain yoghurt, to serve

PREPARATION TIME: **20 MINUTES**
COOKING TIME: **30 MINUTES**

1. Heat the oil in a frying pan or wok and fry the aubergine, turning once to make sure both sides are the same colour. Line a dish with kitchen paper to absorb the excess oil. Place the aubergine slices in the dish as they are cooked. Then fry the potatoes in the same way and add to the lined dish.

2. Fry the whole peppers and chillies, covering the pan with a lid to prevent hot oil spitting.

3. Dip the courgette in a little flour, shake off the excess, and fry until nicely browned. Now transfer all the vegetables to a serving dish.

4. Heat a little oil in a separate frying pan and add the chopped tomatoes and garlic. Fry for a few minutes. Pour this sauce over the vegetables and serve with plain yoghurt. Garnish with chopped parsley.

Stuffing for Vegetables

DOLMA ICI

Here is the basic stuffing recipe for soguk colmalar *'cold stuffed vegetables'.*

Serves 5

PREPARATION TIME: **10 MINUTES**
COOKING TIME: **15 MINUTES**

250 ml/½ pt olive oil
1 large onion, chopped
1 Tbsp pine kernels
200 g/8 oz long grain rice, washed and drained
1 Tbsp small raisins, soaked and washed
Salt and ground black pepper
1 tsp sugar
425 ml/14 fl oz water
Juice of 1 lemon
A handful of fresh parsley, chopped
2 tsp chopped fresh dill
2 tsp chopped fresh mint
1 tsp ground cinnamon

1 Heat the oil in a large saucepan, stir in the onions and pine kernels, and fry for a few minutes, until the kernels are lightly coloured.

2 Add the rice and stir together until the rice becomes transparent. Add the raisins, salt and pepper, sugar, and water to cover. Cover and cook until the water is absorbed.

3 Allow to cool slightly then stir in the lemon juice, parsley, dill and mint.

Cold Stuffed Peppers

ZEYTINYAGLI BIBER DOLMASI

Use any colour pepper you like for this dish. Red and yellow ones are sweeter than green. Or how about a variety for a really eye-catching presentation?

Serves 5

5 peppers
1 quantity stuffing (see above)
1 large fresh tomato, sliced horizontally into 5
Juice of ½ lemon

PREPARATION TIME: **20 MINUTES**
COOKING TIME: **25 MINUTES**

1 Wash the peppers, cut out the stalk and scoop out the seeds. Fill with the stuffing and cover each one with a slice of tomato.

2 Place standing up in a saucepan. The pan should be just big enough to accommodate them yet snug enough to retain their shapes while cooking. Pour a little water into the pan, to a level 5 cm/2 inches below the pepper top, and place a small heatproof plate over the peppers. Cook over medium heat for 15 minutes, until the peppers are softened but still intact. Allow to cool in the saucepan then place in a serving dish and sprinkle with lemon juice.

Cold Stuffed Peppers ▶

Stuffed Vine Leaves

ZEYTINYAGLI YAPRAK DOLMASI

This is a very popular starter although it is quite time consuming. The vine leaves may be fresh or tinned for this dish. You will need the juice of a second lemon and a pinch of salt to prepare fresh leaves.

Serves 4

250 g/9 oz vine leaves, fresh or tinned
1 quantity stuffing (see page 36)
100 ml/¼ pt olive oil
Juice of 1 lemon
1 tsp sugar
Lemon wedges, to serve

PREPARATION TIME: **1 HOUR**
COOKING TIME: **1 HOUR**

1. If using fresh leaves, wash them thoroughly, place in a saucepan, and cover with water. Add the juice of 1 lemon and a pinch of salt. Bring to the boil, cover the pan, and simmer for 20 minutes. If using tinned leaves, wash them and put them in a saucepan with plenty of water. Bring to the boil and simmer for 5 minutes. Allow to cool slightly, drain, and wash again with cold water to remove the excess salt.

2. Place one leaf on a plate, vein side upwards, and put 1 teaspoon of filling in the centre of the leaf near the stem end. Fold the stem end, and then both sides of the leaf over the filling and roll into a cigar shape. Repeat until all the stuffing is used up; you will have some leaves left over.

3. Line the base of a saucepan with the spare leaves, to prevent sticking, and pack stuffed vine leaves in tight layers. Mix the oil with 100 ml/¼ pt water, the sugar and lemon juice, and pour over the stuffed leaves.

4. Cover the *dolmas* with a heatproof plate, to prevent them opening during cooking, and simmer for 1 hour or until tender, adding hot water as it becomes absorbed. Cool in the pan and serve cold with lemon wedges.

Stuffed Cabbage Leaves

ZEYTINYAGLI LAHANA DOLMASI

Although this may seem an unusual way of serving cabbage, it is really quite simple to prepare. It is a very good way of getting children to eat this nutritious vegetable because it is a tasty dish, but remember then to omit the chillies.

Serves 4

1 white or green cabbage, washed
1 quantity stuffing, without mint (see page 36)
Juice of 1 lemon
Salt and ground black pepper
Pinch of paprika or crushed dried red chilli

PREPARATION TIME: **1 HOUR**
COOKING TIME: **40 MINUTES**

1. Cut out the stalk of the cabbage with a sharp knife to give a cone shape, sprinkle with salt and boil rapidly for about 10 minutes in salted water. Once cooled, separate the leaves without tearing. Remove the tough central veins and cut the leaves into hand-size pieces.

2. Line the base of a saucepan with the thick pieces. Place one leaf on a plate, vein side upwards, and place 1 teaspoon of filling in the centre, towards the wider end. Fold the sides over the filling and roll the leaf into a cigar shape. Repeat until all the filling is used up; you will have some leaves left over.

3. Arrange the *dolmas* tightly in the saucepan and cover with a couple of leftover leaves, to prevent leaves coming undone during cooking. Add enough water to cover, bring to the boil, then add the lemon juice, seasoning, and paprika or crushed chilli. Simmer for at least 40 minutes, until tender, adding hot water as it becomes absorbed. Cool in the saucepan

Tip

Choose a cabbage with fresh, crisp leaves. Loosely wrapped, it will keep well in the refrigerator for at least one week.

Mussel Casserole

MIDYE PILAKI

This is a very popular dish in Turkish cuisine. It has a flavour the Turks enjoyed in their Mediterranean empire, where seafood was one of the most accessible and nutritious ingredients.

Serves 4

32 mussels, shelled
Olive oil, for shallow frying
1 onion, chopped
1 carrot, sliced
2 potatoes, peeled and diced
1 celeriac, peeled and diced
2 fresh tomatoes, chopped
2 garlic cloves, crushed
Salt and ground black pepper
Juice of 1 lemon
Chopped fresh parsley, to garnish

PREPARATION TIME: **15 MINUTES**
COOKING TIME: **35 MINUTES**

1. Wash the mussels and cut out the beards with a sharp knife.

2. Heat the oil in a pan and cook the onions until transparent. Add the carrot, potato, celeriac, tomatoes and garlic. Stir-fry for 1 minute, then add 100 ml/¼ pt water. Cover and cook over medium heat for 15 minutes.

3. Add the mussels and cook for 10 minutes more. Season, add the lemon juice, and simmer for 5 minutes. Place in a warm serving dish, garnish with parsley, and serve.

Stuffed Mussels

MIDYE DOLMA

This special dish would be one of the dishes served at the table of many households during any celebratory dinner in Turkey.

Serves 4

250 g/9 oz long grain rice, washed and drained
1 Tbsp pine kernels
1 Tbsp raisins, washed and drained
1 onion, chopped
100 ml/¼ pt olive oil, plus a little extra to glaze
1 tsp sugar
1 tsp dried mint
Salt and ground black pepper
24 large mussels in the shell
Chopped fresh parsley, to garnish

PREPARATION TIME: **40 MINUTES**
COOKING TIME: **30 MINUTES**

1. Mix all the ingredients, except the mussels and parsley, together to make a raw stuffing.

2. Clean the mussels, scraping with a knife. Half open the round part of the shells and, with a pair of kitchen scissors, cut out the beards.

3. Stuff the empty half of the shells with the rice filling and tie a piece of string around each shell to keep them closed.

4. Place the shells in a saucepan with just enough water to cover. Bring to the boil, cover, and simmer for 30 minutes, until the water is absorbed.

5. When cooked, arrange the mussels in layers in a serving dish, cut the strings and brush with a little olive oil. Serve hot, garnished with parsley.

Fried Mussels

MIDYE TAVA

In this delicate dish, mussels are fried in a simple batter and served with lemon juice squeezed over.

Serves 4

32 shelled mussels
10 g/2 oz dried yeast
150 g/5 oz flour
2 eggs, separated
2 Tbsp margarine, melted
1 tsp salt
Olive oil, for shallow frying
Juice of 1 lemon

PREPARATION TIME: **25 MINUTES**
COOKING TIME: **25 MINUTES**

1. Wash the mussels thoroughly, clean off the edges, and dry.

2. In a large mixing bowl, soak the yeast in 2 tablespoons warm water for 10 minutes. Add 125 g/4 oz of the flour, the egg yolks and melted margarine to the yeast mixture and mix well.

3. Whisk the egg whites with the salt, until quite stiff, then fold into the flour paste.

4. Heat some oil in a frying pan. Dip the mussels first in the remaining flour, then into the batter, then fry until golden brown. Place in a serving dish lined with kitchen paper to absorb the excess oil. Drizzle the lemon juice over the mussels and serve.

Tip

When using fresh mussels, check them over carefully and discard any that are open before cooking. They could cause a stomach upset.

Meat and Poultry Dishes

ET YEMEKLERI VE BEYAZ ETLER

Lamb Casserole

KUZU GUVEC

Make sure you have plenty of bread to serve with this dish, to mop up the delicious juices.

Serves 6

15 g/½ oz butter or margarine
1 kg/2 lb tender lamb, diced
500 ml/1 pt meat stock
1 Tbsp tomato purée
12 shallots, peeled
1 garlic clove, crushed
6 cherry tomatoes
2 red peppers, seeded and quartered lengthwise
1 tsp dried or 1 Tbsp chopped fresh thyme
Salt and ground black pepper
Crusty bread, to serve

PREPARATION TIME: **20 MINUTES**
COOKING TIME: **1 HOUR 35 MINUTES**

1. Melt the butter or margarine in a saucepan and add the meat. Fry over high heat for 2 minutes to seal in the juices. Pour the stock over, stir in the tomato purée, and bring to the boil.

2. Add the shallots, garlic, tomatoes and peppers. Mix well, then add the herbs and seasoning.

3. Cover and cook over low heat (or in an oven preheated to 180ºC/350ºF/Gas Mark 4) for 1½ hours, or until the meat is tender and the stock reduced by half. Serve with chunks of warmed bread.

Aubergine Stew

PATLICANLI KEBAP

This is a very pretty stew. The word kebap *in Turkish means that the meat and the aubergines are browned in the frying pan, sealing in the juices.*

Serves 4

4 small aubergines
2 Tbsp olive oil
8 shallots
1 red and 1 green pepper, seeded and cut in chunks
1 chilli, seeded and chopped (optional)
500 g/1 lb mutton
1 Tbsp margarine
1 Tbsp tomato purée
500 ml/1 pt meat stock or water
Salt and ground black pepper
Parsley sprigs, to garnish

PREPARATION TIME: **15 MINUTES**
COOKING TIME: **2 HOURS**

1. Cut each aubergine lengthwise into four pieces and soak in salted water for 20 minutes. Drain and squeeze lightly to extract the excess water.

2. Heat the oil in a frying pan and fry the aubergines lightly, in batches. Set aside when done.

3. In the same oil, fry the shallots, peppers, chilli, if using, and the meat in the same way as the aubergines. Drain and set aside.

4. Melt the margarine in an ovenproof casserole, stir in the tomato purée, then pour in the stock. Bring to the boil, add the meat and vegetables, and season to taste. Cover and cook over low heat for 1½ hours (or alternatively in an oven preheated to 180ºC/350ºF/ Gas Mark 4). Serve hot, garnished with parsley sprigs.

Burgers

KOFTE

These basic kofte *could not be simpler to make. Just mix all the ingredients together, form into burgers, and grill. Alternatively, you can cook them over a barbecue. Serve with French fries and hot pepper sauce, if you like.*

Serves 4

500 g/1 lb ground beef or lamb
1 onion, finely chopped
2 Tbsp fresh breadcrumbs
2 Tbsp chopped fresh parsley
1 tsp ground cumin (optional)
1 egg
Salt and ground black pepper
Olive oil, for brushing

PREPARATION TIME: **30 MINUTES**
COOKING TIME: **25 MINUTES**

1. Mix all the ingredients together in a large bowl with seasoning to taste. Knead thoroughly.

2. Preheat a hot grill. Take walnut-size pieces in your hand and flatten to an oval shape. Continue making little burgers until you have used up all the mixture.

3. Brush the grill rack with a little oil and cook the burgers, turning them for even cooking. Serve hot.

Hasan Pasha Burgers

HASAN PASA KOFTE

These burgers call for twice-minced meat. Ask your butcher to do this for you, or pass the meat through a mincer, or whiz in a blender or food processor at home.

Serves 4

500 g/1 lb minced lamb or beef, minced again
30 g/1 oz fresh breadcrumbs
1 onion, finely chopped
3 eggs
15 g/½ oz butter
3 potatoes
1 Tbsp milk
Salt and ground black pepper
1 Tbsp tomato purée

PREPARATION TIME: **20 MINUTES**
COOKING TIME: **1 HOUR 40 MINUTES**

1. Preheat oven to 190ºC/375ºF/Gas Mark 5. Knead the minced meat in a bowl with the breadcrumbs, onion and two of the eggs, adding a little water if necessary.

2. When thoroughly mixed, take pieces the size of an egg and roll in your wet hands to give an oval shape. Make shallow indentations in the centre of each burger. Place in a large ovenproof dish with half of the butter. Cook in the oven for 25 minutes. When cooked, remove from the oven but leave the oven on.

3. Meanwhile, peel and chop the potatoes and boil in plenty of water. Once cooked, drain and mash.

4. Mix the mashed potato, milk, remaining egg, seasoning and the remaining butter together and place in a saucepan. Cover and cook for about 5 minutes.

5. Fill the indentations in the burgers with the potato mixture. Mix the tomato purée with a little water and pour over the burgers. Place in the oven again for 25 minutes more.

Ladies' Thigh Burgers

KADIN BUDU KOFTE

This kofte is equally good when chilled before serving, making it ideal picnic fare. Its English title is an exact translation from the sixteenth-century Turkish name. I hope you are happy with it!

Serves 4

500 g/1 lb medium lean minced lamb or beef
1 onion, finely chopped
15 g/½ oz butter
50 g/2 oz long grain rice
1 Tbsp chopped fresh parsley
5 eggs
Salt and ground black pepper
1 Tbsp breadcrumbs
Olive oil, for shallow frying

PREPARATION TIME: **20 MINUTES**
COOKING TIME: **1 HOUR**

1. Place two-thirds of the minced meat, the onion and butter in a frying pan and cook until the meat absorbs its own juice.

2. Wash the rice and boil in plenty of water until soft. Drain and set aside.

3. Combine the cooked meat mixture with the remaining raw meat and add the drained rice, parsley, three of the eggs, and salt and pepper. Knead thoroughly, break into pieces the size of a half lemon, and press into an oval shape. Place on a plate, covering each one with breadcrumbs.

4. Whisk the remaining eggs in a bowl big enough to dip the burgers into. Heat some oil in a frying pan and, when hot, dip each burger in the egg, then fry on both sides until cooked through.

Beef with Haricot Beans

ETLI KURU FASULYE

The aroma when cooking this dish is very appetising and the meal itself very satisfying—it is a good one for cold winter evenings. Serve it hot with Rice with Noodles (on page 78).

Serves 4

500 g/1 lb haricot beans
15 g/½ oz butter
1 onion, chopped
1 lb stewing steak, cubed
3 fresh tomatoes, chopped
1 Tbsp tomato purée
1 1/2 pts beef stock or water
1 tsp crushed dried chilli (optional)
1 tsp paprika
Salt and ground black pepper
Boiled rice, to serve

PREPARATION TIME: **OVERNIGHT PLUS 15 MINUTES**
COOKING TIME: **1 HOUR**

1. Soak the beans overnight.

2. The next day, melt the butter and fry the onion until transparent. Add the beef and cook for a few minutes. Then add the tomatoes with the tomato purée.

3. Pour in the stock and bring to the boil. Add the drained beans, crushed chilli, if using, the paprika and seasoning. Cover and cook over medium heat for 1 hour, or until the beans are tender, adding a little more hot water if necessary. Serve hot on a bed of rice.

Doner Kebab

DONER KEBAP

This is the closest you can get to eating an authentic doner kebap *at home. Even in Turkey, many people will go out to eat it in a kebap restaurant. The meat should be tender and, ideally, marinated, and cooked slowly by the upright grill, and then cut into slices. It is traditionally placed on a bed of special bread, called* pide, *and served with a tomato and a butter sauce. The best alternative bread to use is pitta bread or ciabatta bread.*

Serves 4

FOR THE MARINADE

1 Tbsp olive oil
2 tsp plain yoghurt
1 Tbsp tomato purée
2 bay leaves
A few fresh oregano leaves
Salt and ground black pepper

500 g/1 lb lamb, very finely diced
15 g/½ oz butter
2 pita breads or small ciabatta loaves
1 Tbsp tomato purée
2 fresh tomatoes, skinned and chopped
Salt and ground black pepper
1 tsp paprika or crushed dried chillies
200 g/7 oz plain yoghurt

PREPARATION TIME: **10 MINUTES PLUS OVERNIGHT**
COOKING TIME: **30 MINUTES**

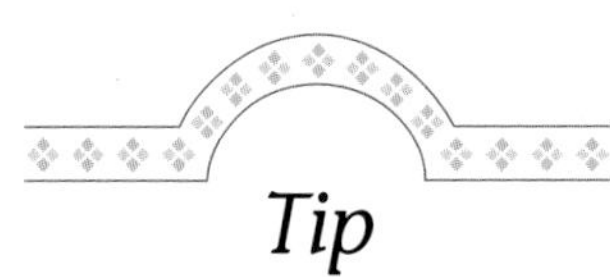

Tip

To skin a tomato, first plunge it into a bowl of boiling water for 1 to 2 minutes and then into a bowl of cold water. The skin will split and you will be able to remove it easily with your fingers.

1. Mix the marinade ingredients in a large bowl and place the lamb pieces in, making sure that they are covered. Cover and chill overnight.

2. The next day, melt half the butter in a frying pan and brown the lamb pieces.

3. Warm the bread under a grill and cut into bite-size pieces. Place on warmed serving plates, then spoon the meat over.

4. Mix the tomato purée with 250 ml/½ pt water and bring to the boil over medium heat. Add the chopped tomatoes and seasoning to taste. Cook until softened. In a separate pan, heat the remaining butter and paprika or chilli.

5. Pour the tomato sauce over the lamb on the plates. Place a spoonful of yoghurt on the side of each plate, then pour the butter sauce over, and serve hot with pickled chillies.

Grilled Lamb on a Skewer

SIS KEBAP

Sis kebap is a very traditional Turkish dish, as popular now as it was with the Nomadic Turkic tribes, from whom this method of cooking meat over an open fire came. Serve hot with aubergine salad and rice.

Serves 4

FOR THE MARINADE

2 large, fresh tomatoes, chopped
2 Tbsp olive oil
2 tsp dried oregano
1 tsp paprika
1 bouquet garni
Salt and ground black pepper

500 g/1 lb lamb, cubed
200 g/7 oz button mushrooms
1 red or green pepper, seeded and cubed
8 bay leaves

PREPARATION TIME: **OVERNIGHT PLUS 15 MINUTES**
COOKING TIME: **30 MINUTES**

1. Mix the marinade ingredients in a large bowl and add the lamb. Stir to coat, then cover, and leave to marinate for at least 6 hours or overnight in the refrigerator.

2. The next day, preheat a hot grill. Arrange the marinated lamb, mushrooms, red or green pepper and bay leaves on eight skewers, alternating the different components.

3. Grill, turning frequently, and brushing with the marinade from time to time. Serve hot, with Rice with Tomatoes (see page 78) and Aubergine Salad (see page 24).

Okra Casserole

ETLI BAMYA

The combination of green okra with the red tomatoes makes this dish very pretty. Try to buy small okra, as they are easier to cook and taste better.

Serves 4

500 g/1 lb okra
Juice of 1½ lemons
25 g/1 oz butter
1 onion, finely chopped
250 g/8 oz stewing lamb or beef
4 fresh plum tomatoes, skinned
Salt and ground black pepper

PREPARATION TIME: **30 MINUTES**
COOKING TIME: **1 HOUR**

1. Cut the stalk out of each okra, leaving a cone-shaped indentation. Wash and soak the okra in a bowl filled with cold water and one-third of the lemon juice for 1 hour.

2. Melt the butter in a saucepan and fry the onions and meat over medium heat. Add the tomatoes, reduce the heat, and simmer for 5 minutes.

3. Wash the okra again before adding to the casserole. Pour just enough water to cover, then cook for about 40 minutes.

4. Add seasoning and the remaining lemon juice, and simmer for 10 minutes more. Serve hot with rice pilaf.

Aubergine Moussaka

PATLICAN MUSAKKA

You can cook this dish using courgettes or potatoes if you prefer. Cook exactly the same way, but for courgette moussaka add some fresh dill. Omit the meat for a vegetarian version.

Serves 4

4 small aubergines
Olive oil, for shallow frying
15 g/½ oz margarine
1 onion, chopped
2 fresh ripe tomatoes, skinned and chopped
8 oz minced lamb or beef
Chopped fresh parsley, to garnish

PREPARATION TIME: **15 MINUTES**
COOKING TIME: **50 MINUTES**

1. Wash the aubergines, peel the skins horizontally in stripes, then slice in circles. Fry the aubergines in a little oil until they change colour. Place in an ovenproof dish.

2. Preheat the oven to 190ºC/375ºF/Gas Mark 5. Heat the margarine in a saucepan, and add the onions, tomatoes and minced meat. Cover and cook for 10 minutes over medium heat.

3. Pour the meat mixture over the aubergines. Add enough water to cover, then cook in the oven for 40 minutes. Serve with chopped parsley scattered over.

Vegetable Casserole

TURLU

Use summer vegetables for a summer casserole or winter ones for a heartier winter stew. You can also use either lamb or beef or simply omit the meat altogether for a vegetarian dish.

Serves 4

2 potatoes, peeled
6 cherry tomatoes
1 carrot, peeled
1 aubergine
1 leek
1 red or green pepper, seeded
1 courgette
25 g/1 oz butter
250 g/8 oz stewing beef
1 onion, chopped
500 ml/1 pt beef stock or water
1 tsp dried oregano
Salt and ground black pepper
Warmed bread rolls, to serve

PREPARATION TIME: **20 MINUTES**
COOKING TIME: **40 MINUTES**

1. Chop the potatoes, tomatoes, carrot, aubergine, leek, red or green pepper and courgette.

2. Heat the butter in a large saucepan. Add the meat and onion, and cook for 10 minutes.

3. Add the prepared vegetables, the stock and the oregano. Cover and cook over medium heat for 30 minutes. When cooked, season to taste, then serve with warmed bread rolls.

Stuffed Aubergine

PATLICAN KARNIYARIK

Such a very simple dish to make, with such delicious results. Serve hot with rice pilaf or hot crusty bread.

Serves 2

1 aubergine
Olive oil, for frying
15 g/½ oz butter or margarine
250 g/7 oz ground beef or lamb
1 onion, chopped
1 Tbsp fresh chopped parsley
1 tsp tomato purée
Salt and ground black pepper
1 tomato, sliced into thin rings

PREPARATION TIME: **30 MINUTES**
COOKING TIME: **30 MINUTES**

1. Peel the skin of the aubergine in stripes. Cut in half lengthwise and scoop out the flesh without breaking the skin. The aubergine halves should look like two boats.

2. Heat a little olive oil in a frying pan and fry the aubergines on all sides until lightly browned. Drain and place in a roasting dish, hollow sides up.

3. Preheat the oven to 190ºC/375ºF/Gas Mark 5. Melt the butter or margarine in a separate pan and cook the meat, onion, parsley and tomato purée together.

4. When cooked, fill the aubergine shells with the meat mixture and place a few tomato rings on each one. Pour 250 ml/½ pt water into the roasting dish. Cook in the oven for 30 minutes, or until the aubergines are cooked. Serve with rice.

Meat Stuffing for Vegetables

ETLI DOLMA ICI

Just as cold stuffed vegetables are popular appetisers, so hot stuffed vegetable dishes are widely offered as a main course. They are quite time consuming to prepare but among them are some of the most delicious of Turkish dishes. Serve with plain yoghurt. The stuffing remains the same with any vegetable so I am giving the basic recipe for stuffing first.

Serves 4

500 g/1 lb minced beef or lamb
1 large onion, finely chopped
2 Tbsp rice, washed
3 Tbsp chopped fresh parsley
1 Tbsp chopped fresh dill (optional)
Salt and ground black pepper
1 Tbsp tomato purée

PREPARATION TIME: **15 MINUTES**

1 In a large bowl knead the minced beef or lamb with the onion, rice, herbs and seasoning.

2 Mix the tomato purée with 3 tablespoons water and add to the meat mixture. Mix again until thoroughly combined.

Stuffed Tomatoes

DOMATES DOLMA

Another favourite in Turkish households, this dish could include red or green peppers, stuffed exactly the same way as the tomatoes, to make a fine presentation of colour and shape. The cooking time is approximate, depending on the firmness of the tomato used. A firm one is better, but simply reduce the cooking time if the tomato is soft as the tomatoes need to stay intact.

Serves 4

1 kg/2 lb large tomatoes
1 quantity stuffing (see above or page 36)
15 g/½ oz butter
1 tsp sugar

PREPARATION TIME: **40 MINUTES**
COOKING TIME: **30 MINUTES**

1 Wash the tomatoes. Cut off the tops with a sharp knife and set aside. Then scoop out the flesh with a teaspoon, being careful not to break the skin, and set aside.

2 Fill each tomato with stuffing and pack firmly in a large saucepan. Cover each one with its own top and pour in 500 ml/1 pt water. Add the butter, sugar and the reserved flesh.

3 Cover and cook for 30 minutes. Serve with garlic or simply plain yoghurt.

Stuffed Tomatoes ▶

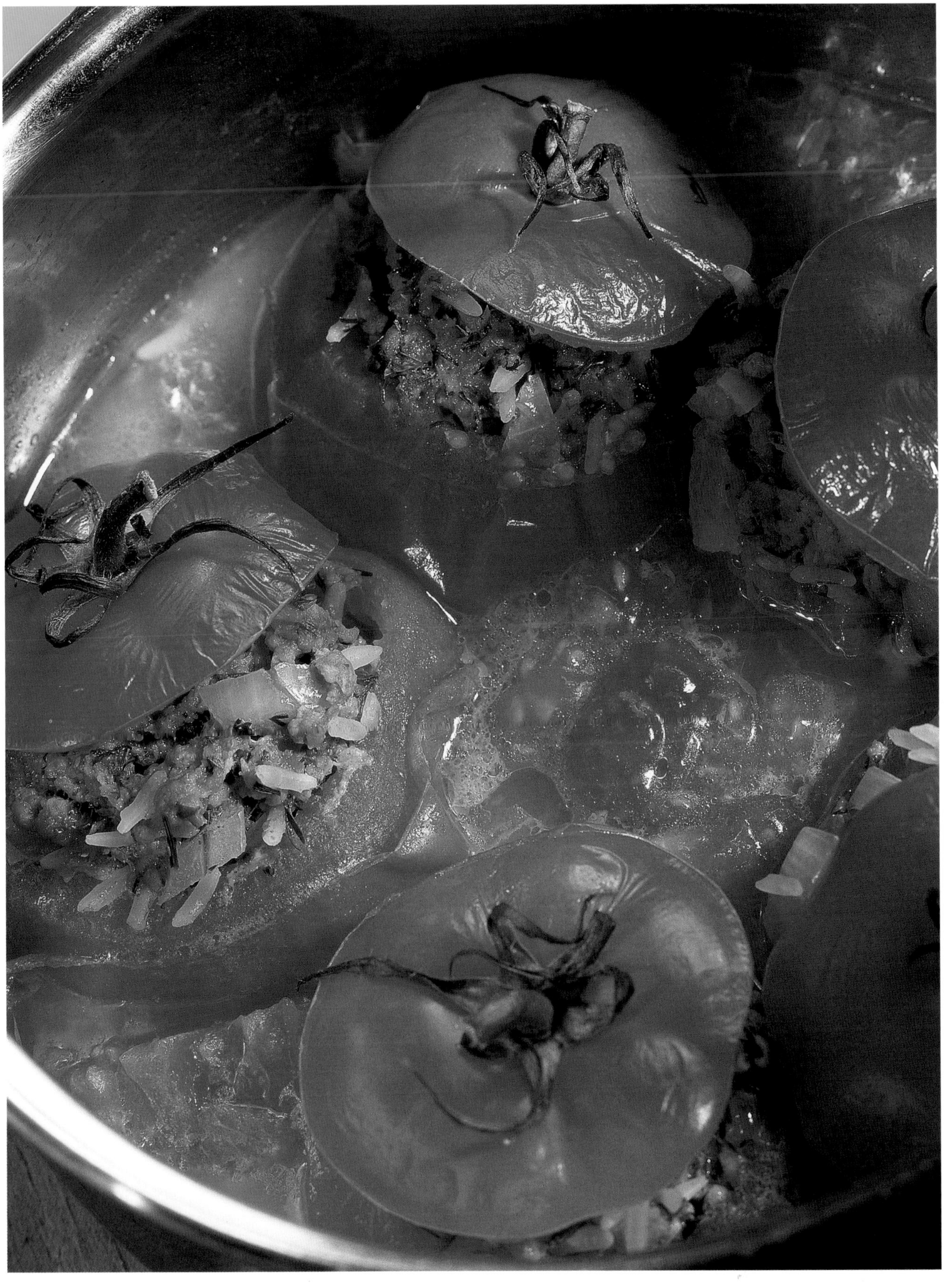

Stuffed Courgettes

ETLI KABAK DOLMA

When you are out shopping for courgette look for plump ones which are easier to hollow out. Keep the scooped-out flesh, covered, in the refrigerator, to use the next day for Fried Courgettes (below).

Serves 4

4 courgettes
1 quantity stuffing (pages 36 and 54)
1 tomato, sliced horizontally
1 tsp tomato purée
15 g/½ oz butter
Garlic yoghurt, to serve

PREPARATION TIME: **40 MINUTES**
COOKING TIME: **40 MINUTES**

1. Wash the courgettes then cut them in half lengthwise. With a teaspoon, scoop the flesh out from inside without tearing the skin.

2. Fill each courgette half quite tightly with the stuffing. Place a tomato ring on each one and pack them firmly in a suitably sized saucepan to prevent them moving while cooking.

3. Add enough water to cover the vegetables, stir in the tomato purée and butter, cover, and cook for 25 minutes over medium heat. Serve hot with garlic yoghurt.

Fried Courgettes

KABAK MUCVERI

If you prepared the Stuffed Courgettes above and kept the scooped-out flesh, use it in this recipe, making up the quantity as necessary.

Tip

To make garlic yoghurt: peel and crush one garlic clove with a little salt. In a bowl, stir the garlic into 250ml/9 fl oz plain yoghurt and serve chilled.

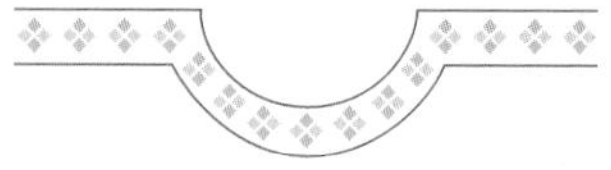

Serves 4

1 Tbsp rice, washed
500 g/1 lb courgettes, peeled and grated
1 Tbsp flour
2 Tbsp chopped fresh dill
2 Tbsp chopped fresh parsley
Salt and ground black pepper
3 eggs
Olive oil, for shallow frying

PREPARATION TIME: **40 MINUTES**
COOKING TIME: **30 MINUTES**

1. Boil the rice in water until soft, drain, and mix with the grated courgettes in a large bowl. Add the flour, dill, parsley, and salt and pepper.

2. Beat the eggs, add to the courgette mixture, and mix well.

3. Heat the oil in a frying pan. Put tablespoonfuls of the mixture into the pan and fry on both sides.

4. As they are cooked, remove them to a serving dish lined with kitchen towels to absorb the excess fat. Serve hot.

Fried Courgettes ▶

Ankara Lamb Roast

ANKARA TAVA

This traditional Turkish meal would often be served when the whole family comes together at holiday times. Serve it hot with new potatoes.

Serves 4

15 g/½ oz butter
1 kg/2 lb boned leg of lamb, cut into 4 pieces
1.2 l/2 pts water or meat stock
1 onion, finely chopped
1 carrot, peeled and diced
100 g/4 oz peas
550 ml/1 pt plain yoghurt
60 g/2 oz flour
Salt and ground black pepper
1 egg
1 tsp paprika

PREPARATION TIME: **20 MINUTES**
COOKING TIME: **1 HOUR**

1. Melt the butter in a pan and fry the lamb pieces until evenly browned. Add the water or stock, the onion, carrot and peas, and bring to the boil. Cover and simmer for 30 minutes.

2. Preheat oven to 190ºC/375ºF/ Gas Mark 5. Transfer the lamb and vegetables to an ovenproof dish, reserving the cooking liquid. Mix 550 ml/1 pint of the liquid with the yoghurt, flour and seasoning to taste. Pour this sauce over the lamb and vegetables.

3. Beat the egg and pour over the dish. Bake for 15 minutes. Sprinkle with the paprika and serve.

Meat and Vegetable Casserole

COMLEK KEBABI

This kebap is usually cooked in an earthenware casserole called a 'Comlek', hence its name. If you are able to use one, cook in a very slow oven for a few hours as this will intensify the flavour and soften the meat. If you are using beef, double the cooking time.

◀ ***Meat and Vegetable Casserole***

Serves 6

15 g/½ oz butter
1 kg/2 lb lamb or beef, diced
6 shallots, peeled
4 oz green beans, sliced
1 aubergine, cubed
2 potatoes, peeled and cubed
2 carrots, peeled and diced
6 cherry tomatoes
60 g/2 oz okra, stems removed
1 chilli, seeded and chopped
1 green pepper, seeded and chopped
1 Tbsp chopped fresh dill
Salt and ground black pepper

PREPARATION TIME: **20 MINUTES**
COOKING TIME: **1½ HOURS**

1. Melt the butter in a heatproof casserole and add the meat.

2. Layer the prepared vegetables over the meat, season with salt and pepper, and scatter over the dill.

3. Add 100 ml/¼ pt water to the casserole, cover, and cook over low heat for 1½ hours, or until the meat is tender.

Lamb Casserole Cooked in Paper

KAGIT KEBABI

Make sure you seal the baking parchment very carefully over the top of each package so they do not come apart in the oven.

Serves 6

30 g/1 oz butter or margarine
1 kg/2 lb lamb, diced
1 onion, chopped
1 carrot, peeled and diced
500 g/1 lb potatoes, peeled and diced
1 fresh tomato, skinned and chopped
100 g/4 oz peas
1 Tbsp tomato purée
1 Tbsp red wine vinegar
2 Tbsp chopped fresh dill
1 tsp dried thyme
Salt and ground black pepper

PREPARATION TIME: **15 MINUTES**
COOKING TIME: **40 MINUTES**

1. Melt the butter or margarine in a saucepan and brown the meat evenly. Add the onion and carrot, cover, and cook until the juices are absorbed.

2. Add the potatoes, tomato, peas, tomato purée dissolved in a little water, and the vinegar. Cook for a few minutes more. Then add 200 ml/⅓ pt water, cover, and cook over low heat for 1 hour.

3. Preheat oven to 190ºC/375ºF/Gas Mark 5. Cut six generous size pieces of baking parchment. Place equal portions of the casserole in the centre of each sheet. Sprinkle the herbs and seasoning over each one. Fold the sides of the papers over the top to make packages. Place the parcels on an ovenproof tray and sprinkle with a little water. Bake in the oven for 20 minutes. Serve in their packages.

Celeriac Casserole

ETLI KEREVIZ

This is a surprisingly simple and delicious casserole. The aroma of celeriac is fresh and appetising.

Serves 2

15 g/½ oz butter
1 onion, finely chopped
500 g/1 lb stewing lamb, cubed
1 small celeriac, peeled and cut into chunks
1 carrot, peeled and chopped
1 Tbsp tomato purée
Juice of 1 lemon
Salt and ground black pepper
Chopped fresh parsley, to garnish

PREPARATION TIME: **15 MINUTES**
COOKING TIME: **25 MINUTES**

1. Melt the butter in a casserole and lightly brown the onion. Add the lamb, cover, and cook until the juices are absorbed, about 3 minutes.

2. Add the celeriac, carrot, tomato purée and lemon juice, along with 250 ml/½ pt water. Stir thoroughly and season.

3. Cook over medium heat for 25 minutes, or until the celeriac is soft but firm. Serve with chopped fresh parsley scattered over.

Lamb Casserole Cooked in Paper ▲

Beef Kebabs

ADANA KEBAP

These are shaped kebabs prepared with minced beef. The beef needs to be quite fatty, so they make an economical yet tasty dish.

Serves 6

1 kg/2 lb fatty minced beef
2 small onions, finely chopped
4 Tbsp chopped fresh parsley
Salt and ground black pepper
Warmed pitta breads, to serve

TO GARNISH

2 onions, thinly sliced
1 garlic clove, crushed
2 Tbsp chopped fresh parsley
A few small tomatoes
3 green peppers, seeded and cut into strips lengthwise

PREPARATION TIME: **30 MINUTES**
COOKING TIME: **45 MINUTES**

1. Place the minced beef in a large bowl with the onions, parsley and seasoning. Knead thoroughly.

2. Preheat a hot grill. Have ready several metal skewers. Take an egg-size piece of the beef mixture in wet hands, and shape it around a skewer, elongating it to a length of about 10 cm/4 inches. Repeat the process with the remaining meat mixture.

3. Place the skewers in the grill pan and grill until cooked through, turning the skewers to ensure even cooking on both sides.

4. Prepare the garnish by mixing the onions with the garlic and parsley. Then lightly grill the tomatoes and green peppers.

5. Serve the beef skewers on warmed pitta breads, garnished with the onion and parsley mixture, and with grilled tomatoes and green peppers on the side.

Beef Ragoût

PAPAZ YAHNISI

This is a very easy dish to prepare. Use good-quality beef and make sure the cubes are about the same size so they cook at the same rate.

Serves 6

15 g/½ oz butter
1 kg/2 lb lean beef, cubed
500 g/1 lb shallots, peeled
3 garlic cloves, crushed
2 Tbsp red wine vinegar
1 tsp cinnamon
1 tsp allspice
Salt and ground black pepper
Warmed bread, to serve

PREPARATION TIME: **15 MINUTES**
COOKING TIME: **2 HOURS**

1. Melt the butter in a large heatproof casserole and cook the beef in its own juices, until browned all over.

2. Add the shallots, garlic, vinegar, spices and seasoning. Pour over 750 ml/1½ pts hot water, cover, and cook over low heat for about 2 hours, or until the meat is tender. Serve hot with warmed bread.

Chicken with Mushrooms

MANTARLI TAVUK

This is a very colourful dish suitable for a family meal and it is delicious served with crusty bread rolls and a green salad.

Serves 4

15 g/½ oz butter or margarine
4 chicken quarters
1 onion, chopped
1 garlic clove, crushed
1 Tbsp flour
450 ml/¾ pt chicken stock
1 Tbsp tomato purée
100 ml/¼ pt dry white wine
1 bouquet garni
3 bay leaves
Salt and ground black pepper
1 red pepper, seeded and chopped
8 oz button mushrooms

PREPARATION TIME: **15 MINUTES**
COOKING TIME: **1½ HOURS**

1. Melt the butter or margarine in a saucepan and fry the chicken portions until evenly browned. Add the onion and garlic, and fry for 2 minutes more, then stir in the flour.

2. Pour in the stock with the tomato purée. Mix well, then add the wine and the herbs. Season to taste, cover, and cook over low heat for 1 hour. Add the red pepper and the mushrooms, and simmer for 15 minutes more before serving.

Poussin Ragoût

PILIC YAHNI

If you cannot get poussins, you could substitute Cornish game hens.

Serves 4

45 g/1½ oz margarine
4 poussins
6 tiny pearl onions, peeled
2 garlic cloves, crushed
2 large fresh tomatoes, chopped
250 ml/½ pt chicken stock or water
100 g/4 oz wild mushrooms
Salt and ground black pepper

PREPARATION TIME: **10 MINUTES**
COOKING TIME: **1½ HOURS**

1. Heat the margarine in a saucepan and add the poussins. Sauté for about 8 minutes, then add the onions, garlic and tomatoes, and fry together for a few minutes more.

2. Add the stock and bring to the boil. Cover and cook over low heat for 1 hour.

3. Add the mushrooms and seasoning, and cook for 20 minutes more. Serve hot on a bed of rice.

Topkapi Palace Chicken

TOPKAPI TAVUK

This dish was developed in the Topkapi Palace kitchens, and is a firm favourite with the Turkish people.

Serves 4

30 g/1 oz butter
1 small fresh chicken, cut into portions
150 g/5 oz chicken livers, chopped
6 shallots, peeled and chopped
1 Tbsp raisins, washed
1 Tbsp pine kernels
1.2 1/2 pts chicken stock
175 g/6 oz long grain rice, washed and drained
Salt and ground black pepper

PREPARATION TIME: **20 MINUTES**
COOKING TIME: **50 MINUTES**

1. Melt half the butter in a frying pan and sauté the chicken pieces until evenly browned. Stir in the liver, shallots and raisins, and fry together for a few minutes more. Transfer to a casserole.

2. Melt the remaining butter in a saucepan and fry the pine kernels until coloured. Add to the casserole.

3. Pour in the stock and bring to the boil. Stir in the drained rice and the seasoning. Cover and cook for 30 minutes over medium heat until all the juice is absorbed and the chicken is tender.

Chicken Burgers

TAVUK KOFTE

These burgers are dipped in flour, egg and then breadcrumbs before frying, which gives them a lovely crisp texture.

Serves 6

30 g/1 oz margarine
3 Tbsp flour
100 ml/¼ pt milk
100 g/4 oz grated Cheddar cheese
3 egg yolks
Salt and ground black pepper
250 g/9 oz cooked chicken, cut into strips
Olive oil, for shallow frying

FOR THE COATING
100 g/4 oz flour
2 eggs
100 g/4 oz fresh breadcrumbs

PREPARATION TIME: **20 MINUTES**
COOKING TIME: **35 MINUTES PLUS CHILLING TIME**

1. Heat the margarine in a saucepan and stir in the flour. Stirring constantly, gradually add the milk. Then, still stirring, add the cheese, egg yolks and seasoning. Cook for 5 minutes, stirring all the time.

2. Turn off the heat and add the chicken. Mix well, then chill for 2 hours.

3. Heat the oil in a frying pan. Sieve the flour onto a plate, whisk the eggs in a good-size bowl, and spread the breadcrumbs out on a second plate.

4. Take walnut-size pieces of the chicken mixture and form into burgers. Dip first into the flour, then into the egg, and, finally, into the breadcrumbs. Fry evenly, drain, and serve.

Seafood Dishes

BALIK YEMEKLERI

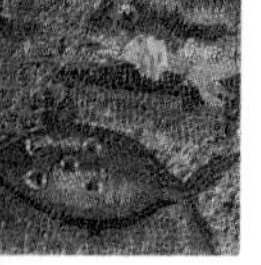

Fish Casserole

BALIK PILAKI

Fish is not known for its colour, but this dish is different and works very well with any type of fish.

Serves 6

1 Tbsp olive oil
1 onion, chopped
1 garlic clove, crushed
1 Tbsp flour
500 ml/1 pt fish stock
1 kg/2 lb fish fillets, such as sea bass or grey mullet
1 potato, peeled
2 carrots, peeled and chopped
2 fresh ripe tomatoes, skinned and chopped
2 bay leaves
Salt and ground black pepper
Juice of ½ lemon
Fresh chopped parsley, to garnish

PREPARATION TIME: **15 MINUTES**
COOKING TIME: **35 MINUTES**

1. Heat the oil in a large saucepan and fry the onions and garlic for a few minutes.

2. Stir in the flour and pour in the stock. Bring to the boil, then add the fish, with the potato, carrot, tomato and bay leaves. Season, cover, and simmer for 20 minutes, or until the potatoes are cooked.

3. Just before serving, sprinkle with lemon juice and parsley.

Prawn Casserole

KARIDES GUVEC

This is a fine alternative way to eat fresh prawns, and is often served, accompanied by chilled white wine, in scallop shells in seaside bars or small restaurants clustered at the harbourside.

Serves 4–6

1 kg/2 lb fresh prawns, shelled and cleaned
Salt and ground black pepper
2 Tbsp olive oil
1 Spanish onion, chopped
1 garlic clove, crushed
2 fresh tomatoes, skinned and chopped
1 green or red pepper, seeded and chopped
1 chilli, seeded and chopped
150 g/5 oz grated Cheddar cheese

PREPARATION TIME: **20 MINUTES**
COOKING TIME: **35 MINUTES**

1. Preheat oven to 220ºC/425ºF/Gas Mark 7. Sprinkle the prawns with a pinch of salt. Heat the oil in a saucepan and lightly brown the onion and garlic. Turn off the heat.

2. In a large bowl, mix the prawns with the tomatoes, green or red pepper, chilli and seasoning. Add the onion mixture.

3. Divide the mixture into portions, place in individual ovenproof dishes, and scatter over the Cheddar cheese.

4. Bake in the middle of the oven for 15 minutes, until cooked through and bubbling and golden on top.

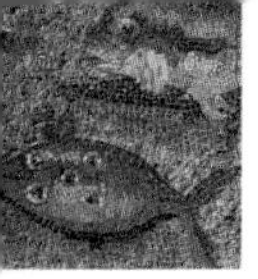

Anchovy Rice

HAMSILI PILAV

The people of the Black Sea region are famous for the ways they use fresh anchovies to create surprisingly delicious dishes. Even if you cannot find anchovies you can also use whitebait which is widely available. The cleaning of this fish takes time but it is well worth the effort.

Serves 4

FOR THE PILAF

250 g/9 oz long grain rice
30 g/1 oz butter
400 ml/¾ pt chicken stock

500 g/1 lb fresh anchovies
1 large Spanish onion, cut into rings
1 large fresh tomato, sliced horizontally
1 green or red pepper, sliced
Lemon wedges, to serve

PREPARATION TIME: **1 HOUR**
COOKING TIME: **1 HOUR**

1. Place the rice in a bowl and cover with hot water. Allow to cool, then drain, wash thoroughly, and drain again.

2. Melt the butter in a saucepan, add the stock, and bring to the boil. Add the rice, cover, and simmer for 5 minutes. Then reduce the heat and simmer for 15 minutes more, or until the liquid is completely absorbed.

3. Preheat oven to 180ºC/350ºF/ Gas Mark 4. Wash the fish under cold running water and separate the bones by cutting the side of the fish halfway through from the head and pulling the bone out.

4. Line a large ovenproof dish with half of the rice then place the onion and half the fish on top. Cover with the rest of the rice, fish, and tomato and pepper slices in layers.

5. Cook in the oven for 20 minutes. Serve hot, with lemon wedges for squeezing over.

Skewered Swordfish

KILIC SIS

Tasty and elegant, this dish is suitable for a small dinner party. The fish will remain intact during cooking and the flavour is very subtle. Serve hot with crusty white bread.

Serves 4

FOR THE MARINADE

1 Tbsp olive oil
1 Tbsp lemon juice
1 Tbsp salt
1 tsp paprika
6 bay leaves
Ground black pepper

500 g/1 lb swordfish, washed and cut into chunks
1 red onion, peeled and cut into chunks
1 green pepper, cut into bite-size pieces
Green salad leaves, to serve
Juice of 1 lemon, for sprinkling
A few radishes, to garnish

PREPARATION TIME: **30 MINUTES PLUS OVERNIGHT**
COOKING TIME: **20 MINUTES**

1 Mix the marinade ingredients together in a bowl large enough to accommodate the swordfish pieces. Add the fish and leave, covered, in the refrigerator for at least 6 hours.

2 Preheat a hot grill. Thread the fish, onion and pepper pieces onto metal skewers alternately. Grill for 5 minutes on each side, brushing occasionally with the marinade mixture.

3 Serve hot, on a bed of lettuce leaves, sprinkled with lemon juice, and garnished with radishes.

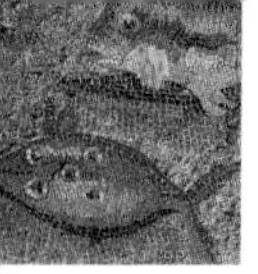

Fried Turbot

KALKAN TAVA

This is a very delicious fish which certainly does not require serving with a sauce. It is absolutely well worth getting if you can find it fresh. When it is simply fried and served with a crisp green salad it will make a lovely Sunday lunch.

Serves 4

1 kg/2 lb fresh turbot
250 ml/½ pt olive oil
50 g/2 oz flour
Salt and ground black pepper
Juice of 1 lemon
2 Tbsp chopped fresh parsley

PREPARATION TIME: **20 MINUTES**
COOKING TIME: **30 MINUTES**

1. If the fish is whole, first cut it into portions, then wash the portions thoroughly.

2. About 20 minutes before serving, heat the oil in a large frying pan and mix the flour and seasoning together on a plate.

3. Dip the fish portions into the flour, making sure they are coated all over. Shake off the excess and fry until golden brown, turning once. Drain and place the portions in a warmed serving dish. Serve hot with lemon juice and parsley scattered over.

Skewered Prawns

KARIDES SIS

Dublin Bay prawns, Tiger prawns or langoustine can be used for this dinner party dish. It is important not to overcook the fish.

Serves 4

20 or 24 fresh prawns, shelled
Juice of ½ lemon
2 fresh tomatoes
1 green pepper
6 bay leaves
1 lemon, sliced into rings
Salt and ground black pepper
1 Tbsp olive oil
Mixed salad leaves and boiled new potatoes, to serve

PREPARATION TIME: **30 MINUTES**
COOKING TIME: **20 MINUTES**

1. Wash and drain the prawns, brush with lemon juice, and set aside.

2. Cut the tomatoes and green pepper into bite-size pieces, and halve the bay leaves.

3. Preheat a hot grill. Thread the prawns, tomato and green pepper pieces, halved bay leaves, and lemon rings alternately onto four metal skewers.

4. Grill for 5 to 7 minutes on each side, brushing with the olive oil seasoned with salt and pepper. Serve hot with mixed salad leaves and boiled new potatoes.

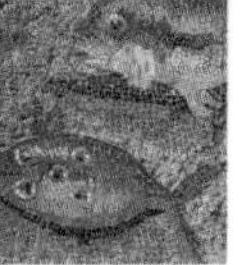

Bonito with Sauce

SOSLU PALAMUT

You can use any big fish for this dish. The sauce transforms even the dullest. Serve it with a mixed leaf salad and warmed bread.

Serves 4

1 large fish
1 carrot, peeled and sliced
1 onion, chopped
½ a small celeriac, peeled and sliced
4 bay leaves
Juice of ½ lemon
Salt and ground black pepper

FOR THE SAUCE
300 g/10 oz cornflour
4 egg yolks
Juice of 1 lemon
Salt
150 g/5 oz butter

PREPARATION TIME: **20 MINUTES**
COOKING TIME: **50 MINUTES**

1. Place the fish, carrot, onion, celeriac, bay leaves and lemon juice in a large saucepan. Add salt and pepper to taste.
2. Cover with a little water and bring to the boil. Simmer for 25 to 30 minutes, then arrange the fish in a warmed serving dish.
3. For the sauce, place the flour, egg yolks and lemon juice in a saucepan over medium heat. Stirring slowly, gradually add 400 ml/¾ pt water. Mix thoroughly, add salt, and keep on stirring until the sauce thickens. Turn the heat off, then add the butter, stirring until blended.
4. Pour the sauce over the fish and serve immediately.

Sea Bass with Raki Sauce

RAKI SOSLU LEVREK

Raki *is a strong spirit distilled from grain in Turkey, and flavoured with aniseed and other aromatics. If you cannot find it, substitute the French apéritif, Pernod.*

Serves 4

30 g/1 oz butter
1 Spanish onion, peeled and chopped
1 large fresh tomato, chopped
4 large sea bass steaks
4 Tbsp dry white wine
Salt and ground black pepper
2 Tbsp double cream
4 Tbsp *raki* or Pernod
Chopped fresh parsley and dill, to garnish

PREPARATION TIME: **10 MINUTES**
COOKING TIME: **45 MINUTES**

1. Melt the butter in a saucepan and fry the onion until soft.
2. Add the tomato and the fish steaks, and pour in water just to cover. Stir in the wine and seasoning. Bring to the boil, cover, and cook over low heat for 20 minutes. Then place the fish steaks in a warmed serving dish, leaving the stock in the saucepan.
3. Heat the stock and stir in the double cream and *raki* or Pernod. Pour the sauce over the fish and serve garnished with the parsley and dill.

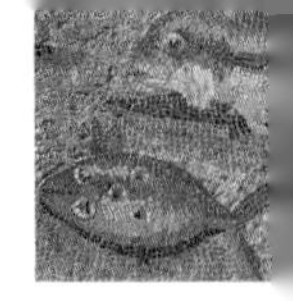

Sea Bass with **Raki** *Sauce* ▲

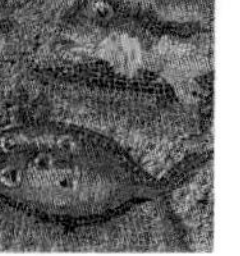

Fish with Onions and Tomatoes

SOGANLI DOMATESLI BALIK

This is a very easy dish to make and tastes delicious.

Serves 4

500 g/1 lb red mullet or mackerel
1 Tbsp olive oil
2 onions, sliced into rings
4 fresh tomatoes, skinned
1 lemon, sliced
4 bay leaves
Salt and ground black pepper
Boiled new potatoes, to serve

PREPARATION TIME: **15 MINUTES**
COOKING TIME: **45 MINUTES**

1. Preheat oven to 190ºC/375ºF/Gas Mark 5. Arrange the fish carefully in a large ovenproof dish.

2. Heat the olive oil in a frying pan and fry the onions and tomatoes gently for a few minutes. Pour over the fish with enough water to cover.

3. Place the lemon rings and the bay leaves on top of the onion mixture, season, and cook in the oven for 30 minutes. Serve hot with boiled new potatoes.

Steamed Fish

BALIK BUGULAMA

Sardines and anchovies combine to produce a delicate flavour that tastes wonderful with new potatoes and butter.

Serves 4

1 kg/2 lb fresh sardines or anchovies
1 onion, very finely chopped
1 Tbsp chopped fresh dill
1 Tbsp chopped fresh parsley
Salt and ground black pepper
750 ml/½ pt fish stock
Lemon wedges, to serve

PREPARATION TIME: **25 MINUTES**
COOKING TIME: **30 MINUTES**

1. Wash the fish and arrange in a large saucepan in alternate layers with the onion and herbs. Add seasoning to taste and pour in the stock.

2. Bring to the boil, cover, and simmer for 8 to 10 minutes. Serve with lemon wedges for squeezing over.

Rice and Pasta Dishes

PILAVLAR VE MAKARNALAR

Rice with Noodles

SEHRIYELI PILAV

In Turkish cuisine, it is not unusual to serve a dish of rice combined with noodles. This is a very basic dish and is suitable for serving with just about any main course dish.

Serves 6

400 g/1 lb long grain rice, washed and drained
15 g/½ oz butter
750 ml/1½ pt chicken stock
1 Tbsp or a good handful of noodles
Salt and ground black pepper

PREPARATION TIME: **5 MINUTES**
COOKING TIME: **35 MINUTES**

1. Soak the rice in hand-hot water, allow to cool, then drain.

2. Heat the butter in a saucepan and add the chicken stock. When it is boiling, add the rice and noodles. Stir once, season, and cover. Cook over medium heat until the liquid is absorbed, reducing the heat for the last 5 minutes.

Pasta with Mushrooms

MANTARLI MAKARNA

Wild mushrooms are used in this dish. They are now more widely available in supermarkets but you could substitute common cultivated ones if you wish.

Serves 4

250 ml/½ pt meat stock
200 g/7 oz wild mushrooms, wiped and chopped
15 g/½ oz butter plus a little extra
Salt and ground black pepper
200 g/7 oz roast beef, chopped
1 small onion, chopped
2 fresh tomatoes, chopped
1 Tbsp tomato purée
250 g/9 oz spaghetti
60 g/2 oz Cheddar cheese, grated

PREPARATION TIME: **15 MINUTES**
COOKING TIME: **1 HOUR 45 MINUTES**

1. Bring the meat stock to the boil and stir in the mushrooms, butter, and salt and pepper. Simmer for 10 minutes, remove the mushrooms from the pan, and set aside the mushrooms and the stock.

2. Heat a knob of butter in a frying pan and stir in the roast beef, onion, tomatoes, tomato purée and the stock from the mushrooms. Cover and cook for 30 minutes, adding hot water when necessary.

3. Cook the pasta according to the package instructions, drain, then place in a large serving dish.

4. Add the mushrooms to the sauce, cook for 5 minutes more, then pour over the pasta with the grated cheese. Serve immediately.

Sultan Resat Rice

SULTAN RESAT PILAVI

As the name suggests, this is a traditional Ottoman dish that has stood the test of time. In the Ottoman Empire, the Sultan's corps of soldiers, the Jannissaries, would have one huge cauldron especially for the pilaf. When they revolted, a not uncommon event, the first sign of the upheaval would be the overturned pilaf cauldron.

Serves 6

400 g/1 lb long grain rice, washed and drained
30 g/1 oz butter
750 ml/1½ pts chicken stock or water
200 g/8 oz minced beef or lamb
1 bread slice, crusts removed, crumbed
1 onion, finly chopped
15 g/½ oz margarine
1 Tbsp tomato purée
Salt and ground black pepper

PREPARATION TIME: **15 MINUTES**
COOKING TIME: **1 HOUR 10 MINUTES**

1. Soak the rice in hand-hot water, allow to cool, and drain.

2. Heat the butter in a saucepan, pour in the stock, and bring to the boil. Add the rice, cover, and cook over medium heat for 15 minutes. Then reduce the heat and simmer for 10 minutes more, until the liquid is absorbed. Keep warm.

3. Knead the minced meat with the breadcrumbs and onion. Take walnut-size pieces of the mixture and, with wet hands, roll into balls.

4. Heat the margarine in a frying pan and fry the meatballs evenly. Add 100 ml/¼ pt water, stir in the tomato purée, and season to taste. Cover and cook until the meatballs are tender.

5. Place the rice in a serving dish, make hollow in the centre, and pour in the meatballs and sauce.

Rice with Chicken Livers and Raisins

IC PILAV

This rice is usually prepared to eat with poultry and is cooked with poultry liver. Chestnuts are also added to the dish when it is served at New Year celebrations.

Serves 6

50 g/2 oz pine kernels
50 g/2 oz raisins
15 g/½ oz butter
100 g/4 oz chicken or turkey liver, chopped
2 fresh tomatoes, skinned and chopped
750 ml/1½ pts chicken stock
400 g/1 lb long grain rice, washed and drained
Salt and ground black pepper

PREPARATION TIME: **20 MINUTES**
COOKING TIME: **50 MINUTES**

1. Wash the pine kernels and raisins then dry.

2. Heat half the butter in a small pan and fry the pine kernels until they change colour. Add the raisins and the liver and cook for 3 minutes.

3. Heat the remaining butter in a saucepan and fry the tomatoes for 2 minutes, then pour in the stock, and bring to the boil.

4. Drain the chicken livers, pine kernels and raisins, and transfer to the tomato mixture. Add the rice and seasoning to taste. Cover and cook over medium heat for 30 minutes, until the liquid is absorbed.

5. Allow to rest for 5 minutes over very low heat, before serving with a turkey or chicken dish.

Rice with Tomatoes

DOMATESLI PILAV

This is again one of the simplest ways of cooking rice but it tastes very good. It is served as a side dish with grilled or barbecued meat or sausages.

Serves 6

400 g/1 lb long grain rice, washed and drained
30 g/1 oz butter
3 fresh ripe tomatoes, skinned and chopped
750 ml/1½ pts chicken stock
1 tsp tomato purée
Salt and ground black pepper

PREPARATION TIME: **5 MINUTES**
COOKING TIME: **40 MINUTES**

1. Soak the rice in hand-hot water, allow to cool, and drain.

2. Heat the butter in a saucepan and fry the tomatoes for a few minutes. Pour the chicken stock over and bring to the boil.

3. Add the rice, stir in the tomato purée, and season to taste.

4. Cover and cook over medium heat for 15 minutes, then reduce the heat, and simmer for 10 minutes more, until the liquid is absorbed.

Rice with Prawns

KARIDESLI PILAV

This pilaf is a meal in itself, simple to make and very nutritious.

Serves 6

250 g/9 oz shelled prawns, fresh or frozen
15 g/½ oz butter
750 ml/1½ pts chicken stock or water
400 g/1 lb long grain rice, washed and drained
Salt and ground black pepper
50 g/2 oz cooked peas
Chopped fresh parsley, to garnish

PREPARATION TIME: **10 MINUTES**
COOKING TIME: **30 MINUTES**

1. If using fresh prawns, boil in salted water with 1 tablespoon white wine vinegar for 3 minutes.

2. Melt the butter in a saucepan and pour in the stock. Bring to the boil and add the rice. Season, cover, and cook over medium heat until the liquid is absorbed, about 20 minutes.

3. Line a ring mould with cling film and place half the prawns in the base, then half the rice over the prawns, then the peas, and the rice again. Finish off with a layer of prawns and rice. Pack the ingredients firmly into the mould.

4. To serve, invert the mould onto a serving dish and garnish with parsley.

Istanbul-style Pilaf

ISTANBUL PILAV

When in Istanbul... This popular dish in that city is very filling, so it is best served by itself or with a lightly grilled chicken breast.

Serves 4

15 g/½ oz butter
500 g/1 lb long grain rice, washed and drained
A pinch of saffron, finely crushed
750 ml/1½ pts chicken stock
1 Tbsp blanched almonds
200 g/7 oz petit pois
2 chicken livers or 1 chicken breast, cooked and chopped
Salt and ground black pepper
1 Tbsp shelled pistachios

PREPARATION TIME: **20 MINUTES**
COOKING TIME: **1 HOUR**

1. Heat the butter in a saucepan and add the rice. Cook for 5 minutes, stirring constantly.

2. Soak the saffron in about 2 tablespoons boiling water for 5 minutes. Pour over the rice with the stock. Stir, then add the almonds, petit pois, chicken liver or breast, and seasoning.

3. Stir again, cover, and cook for about 30 minutes. When cooked, leave the pilaf to rest over very low heat for 5 minutes, stir in the pistachios, and serve.

Pasta with Yoghurt

YOGURTLU MAKARNA

Use any type of pasta shape you like for this dish.

Serves 4

500 g/1 lb fresh or no pre-cook pasta
Salt and ground black pepper
A few drops of olive oil
15 g/½ oz butter plus a little extra
1 onion, chopped
200 g/7 oz minced beef or lamb
250 g/9 oz plain yoghurt
2 garlic cloves, crushed
1 tsp paprika
1 tsp dried mint

PREPARATION TIME: **15 MINUTES**
COOKING TIME: **30 MINUTES**

1. Place the pasta in a saucepan of boiling water, with a little salt and a few drops of olive oil to prevent sticking. Cook for 10 minutes, or until the pasta is tender, then drain.

2. Heat the butter in a frying pan and stir in the onion and meat. Cook, stirring continuously, until the meat juices are absorbed. Season to taste.

3. Place one quarter of the pasta in the base of a serving dish. Cover with one-third of the meat mixture. Repeat twice more, then end with a layer of pasta.

4. Mix the yoghurt with garlic, and pour this over the pasta, spreading evenly. Heat a knob of butter in a frying pan, stir in the paprika, then pour over the pasta as well. Serve hot with the mint scattered over.

Cracked Wheat Pilaf

BULGUR PILAVI

This is a very healthy dish and it tastes delicious. You can find cracked wheat in health-food stores and some supermarkets. There are two types of wheat on sale now. One is very thin wheat which is used in salads, koftes and some soups, and does not require cooking. For this recipe the thicker cracked wheat is used.

Serves 4

30 g/1 oz butter
1 onion, finely chopped
1 fresh tomato, finely chopped
1 mild chilli or green pepper, finely chopped
250 g/9 oz cracked wheat
1.2 l/2 pts hot chicken stock or water
1 Tbsp tomato purée
Salt and ground black pepper

PREPARATION TIME: **10 MINUTES**
COOKING TIME: **25 MINUTES**

1. Melt the butter in a saucepan and fry the onion until translucent. Add the tomato and chilli or green pepper, and, stirring continuously, cook for a few minutes.

2. Add the cracked wheat, season, and stir over high heat for 1 minute.

3. Pour over the hot chicken stock or water, stir in the tomato purée, and season with salt and pepper. Cook over medium heat until the liquid is absorbed.

4. Allow to rest over very low heat for 5 minutes before serving.

Fresh Pasta Drops

MANTI

This is a very famous dish from the Black Sea region. It is actually quite similar to tortellini and is traditionally served with garlic yoghurt and a dash of melted butter with paprika. It is a time-consuming dish but with absolutely wonderful results. Serve with a light appetiser because it is quite filling.

Serves 4

450 g/1 lb plain flour
1 large egg
Salt and ground black pepper
250 g/9 oz minced beef or lamb
1 onion, finely chopped
1 Tbsp chopped fresh parsley
Butter, for brushing
Hot beef stock or water

FOR THE SAUCE

400 ml/1 pt plain yoghurt
1 garlic clove, crushed
30 g/1 oz butter
1 tsp paprika or crushed dried chilli
1 tsp dried mint

PREPARATION TIME: **1 HOUR PLUS 1 HOUR STANDING TIME**
COOKING TIME: **55 MINUTES**

1. Sieve the flour and ½ teaspoon salt into a large bowl and make a hollow in the centre. Knead with the egg, and sufficient water to a smooth, workable dough. Cover with a wet cloth and leave for 1 hour.

2. Sprinkle the work surface with flour and roll the dough out into a small circle. Gradually increasing the size of the circle, roll it as thin as possible to a thickness of 3 or 4 mm/⅛ inch. Cut the pastry into 5-cm/2-inch squares.

3. Preheat oven to 190ºC/375ºF/Gas Mark 5. Mix together the minced meat, onion, parsley, and salt and pepper. Place 1 teaspoon of this mixture in the centre of a pastry square. Bring the corners of the square together over the top of the filling and squeeze with your fingers to stick firmly. Repeat with the rest of the squares.

4. Arrange the packages in a deep ovenproof dish and brush with a little butter. Bake in the oven for 25 minutes, until lightly browned. Now pour over just enough hot stock or water to come halfway up the *manti*. Return to the oven and cook for about 30 minutes more, or until the liquid is absorbed. Place the *manti* in a warmed serving dish.

5. Mix the yoghurt with garlic and pour over the pastries. In a small frying pan, melt the butter and stir in the paprika or crushed chilli. Stir for 1 minute then pour over the *manti* as well. Serve hot with dried mint scattered over.

Pasta with Leeks

PIRASALI MAKARNA

Leeks and bacon complement each other wonderfully in this delicious pasta bake.

Serves 4

250 g/9 oz tagliatelli
2 leeks, chopped
6 bacon slices, grilled
3 eggs
250 ml/9 fl. oz plain yoghurt
Salt and ground black pepper
200 g/7 oz Cheddar cheese, grated

PREPARATION TIME: **10 MINUTES**
COOKING TIME: **30 MINUTES**

1. Cook the pasta, then drain. Simmer the leeks in water until tender.

2. Preheat oven to 200ºC/400ºF/ Gas Mark 6. Line an ovenproof dish with the bacon, then place the pasta and the leeks in layers, finishing with a layer of pasta.

3. Whisk the eggs into the yoghurt, and add salt and pepper. Spread over the pasta. Scatter the cheese evenly over the top. Cook in the oven for 25 minutes. Serve hot.

Pasta in the Oven

FIRINDA MAKARNA

The pasta used in this recipe is a speciality of the Black Sea region, and it is similar to spaghetti, but it is 3 mm/⅛ inch in diameter. You can usually find it in good delicatessens, but spaghetti is a good substitute.

Serves 4

500 g/1 lb dried spaghetti
Salt and ground black pepper
A few drops of olive oil
30 g/1 oz butter
200 g/7 oz Cheddar cheese, grated
3 eggs
500 ml/1 pt milk

PREPARATION TIME: **5 MINUTES**
COOKING TIME: **1 HOUR**

1. Place the pasta in a saucepan of boiling water, with a little salt and a few drops of olive oil to prevent sticking. Cook for 15 minutes, or until the pasta is tender, then drain.

2. Preheat oven to 200ºC/400ºF/ Gas Mark 6. Place the pasta in a deep ovenproof dish and mix well with the butter and half the cheese. Scatter the remaining cheese on top.

3. Beat the eggs with the milk, and salt and pepper. Pour over the pasta, spreading evenly. Cook in the oven for 25 minutes. Cut into squares and serve hot.

Rose Pasta

GUL MANTI

These manti *are named for their appearance rather than the inclusion of rose water. They are a little awkward to make but look so attractive that the extra effort is worthwhile.*

Serves 4

175 g/6 oz minced beef or lamb
1 onion, finely chopped
30 g/1 oz chopped fresh parsley
Salt and ground black pepper
300 g/10 oz filo pastry, fresh or frozen
1 egg yolk, for brushing
Garlic yoghurt, to serve

PREPARATION TIME: **1 HOUR**
COOKING TIME: **25 MINUTES**

1. Place the meat in a bowl with the onion, parsley and seasoning. Mix well.

2. Preheat oven to 180ºC/350ºF/ Gas Mark 4. On a floured surface, cut the filo pastry into large triangles. Place 1 tablespoon of the meat mixture in the centre of one side of a triangle. Fold over the two corners and roll like a cigar. Then, starting from one end, roll the cigar shape into a rose shape, sticking the end with a little water. Repeat with all the triangles.

3. Brush the *manti* with egg yolk and bake in the oven for 25 minutes, until golden. Place in a serving dish and pour over the garlic yoghurt.

Tip

Filo pastry dries out very quickly and becomes unworkable. To prevent this, keep the pastry sheets under a damp tea towel, and only take out one at a time. Any leftover pastry can be rolled up, sealed in a freezer bag, and kept in the freezer.

Spinach Pie
ISPANAKLI BOREK

Cheese Pie
PEYNIRLI BOREK

Raw Pie
CIG BOREK

Cheese Rolls
PUACA

Puff Pie
PUF BOREK

Water Pie
SU BOREGI

Talas Pie
TALAS BOREK

Savoury Pies BOREKLER

Spinach Pie

ISPANAKLI BOREK

This is a very good way to make children eat spinach. It is easy to make, especially if you use ready-made pastry. You can either use filo or puff pastry, but with filo pastry it is quite crispy.

Serves 4

30 g/1 oz butter
1 onion, finely chopped
1 kg/2 lb fresh spinach leaves, washed and chopped
Salt and ground black pepper
500 g/1 lb puff pastry
A little melted butter
300 g/10 oz feta cheese, cubed
1 egg yolk, for brushing

PREPARATION TIME: **30 MINUTES**
COOKING TIME: **45 MINUTES**

1. Melt the butter in a large frying pan, fry the onions until soft, then add the spinach. (It may seem quite a lot to begin with but, once cooked, the spinach will reduce.) Cook for a few minutes, stir in seasoning to taste, drain, and set aside.

2. Preheat oven to 190ºC/375ºF/ Gas Mark 5. On a floured surface, roll out half the pastry as thin as possible to line a 30-cm/12-inch square, deep ovenproof dish. Brush the dish with a little melted butter and sprinkle with flour. Line the dish with the pastry and fill first with the cheese cubes then with the spinach and onion mixture.

3. Roll out the remaining pastry to a square large enough to cover the dish, place over the filling, and seal the edges with a little water.

4. Brush the pie with half the egg yolk and cook in the oven for 25 minutes, until nicely browned. Remove from the oven, turn the pie over and brush again with the remaining egg yolk, then return to the oven for 20 minutes more. Serve hot.

Tip

If you like, add four or five cooked bacon slices for a different taste. You can also substitute canned spinach for the fresh, but drain it very thoroughly.

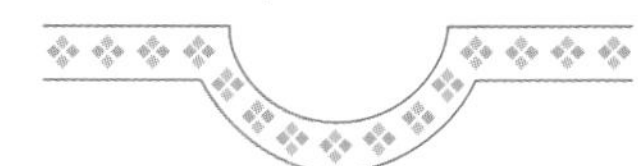

Cheese Pie

PEYNIRLI BOREK

Besides feta cheese, you could also use different ingredients for this pie. For example, cooked minced meat with herbs, or cooked chicken pieces in cream.

Serves 4

6 sheets filo pastry
15 g/½ oz butter
1 Tbsp plain yoghurt
2 eggs
500 g/1 lb feta cheese
60 g/2 oz chopped fresh parsley
1 tsp chilli powder or paprika
Salt and ground black pepper

PREPARATION TIME: **30 MINUTES**
COOKING TIME: **25 MINUTES**

1. Preheat oven to 190ºC/375ºF/ Gas Mark 5. Grease an ovenproof dish, and line with one of the filo pastry sheets.

2. Mix the butter, eggs and yoghurt together in a bowl. Brush a little of this mixture onto the filo pastry. Place another sheet on top and brush with the mixture again, then repeat.

3. Mash the cheese in a separate bowl with the parsley, chilli powder or paprika, and salt and pepper. Spread this mixture evenly over the pastry in the dish.

4. Sandwich the remaining pastry sheets with the egg mixture on top of the filling. Brush the top sheet as well, then cook in the oven for 25 to 30 minutes. Serve hot.

Raw Pie

CIG BOREK

This is a very light, crisp and tasty borek. *You may cook the minced meat beforehand if you do not want to use it raw.*

Serves 4

250 g/9 oz minced beef or lamb
1 onion, finely chopped
1 tsp tomato purée
Salt and ground black pepper
250 g/9 oz plain flour
1 egg
Olive oil, for shallow frying

PREPARATION TIME: **1 HOUR**
COOKING TIME: **20 MINUTES**

1. Knead the minced meat in a bowl with the onion, tomato purée and salt and pepper.

2. Sieve the flour onto the work surface, make a well in the centre, and break the egg into it. Add salt and knead to a medium-soft dough, adding a little water if necessary. Divide the dough into balls about half the size of a lemon, place a damp tea towel over the balls, and allow to rest for 20 minutes.

3. Roll each ball out to a 10-cm/ 4-inch circle. Place 1 teaspoon of filling in one half of the circle, fold the other half over the top, and seal the edges with a little water. Heat the oil in a frying pan and, when hot, fry the pastries evenly, turning once. Drain and serve hot.

Cheese Rolls

PUACA

These little pastries can be made in advance as they keep well. They can be reheated the next day without losing their flavour.

Serves 4

125 g/5 oz margarine
1 egg
100 g/4 oz plain yoghurt
2 tsp baking powder
375 g/12 oz plain flour
250 g/9 oz feta cheese
30 g/1 oz chopped fresh parsley
1 tsp paprika
1 tsp ground black pepper
1 egg yolk
Sesame or poppy seeds, for sprinkling

PREPARATION TIME: **50 MINUTES**
COOKING TIME: **30 MINUTES**

1. Melt the margarine and, when cooled, beat with the egg, yoghurt, and baking powder. Add the flour and knead to a soft dough.

2. Mash the cheese with the parsley, paprika and black pepper.

3. Preheat oven to 200ºC/400ºF/ Gas Mark 6. Take walnut-size pieces of the pastry and, on a floured surface, flatten them into 5-cm/ 2-inch circles. Place the filling on one half of a circle and fold the other half over the top to make a crescent shape. Cut round the edges of the shape with a pastry cutter to smooth the edges and seal. Repeat until all the pastry is used up.

4. Brush each roll with egg yolk and sprinkle with sesame or poppy seeds. Place on a greased baking sheet and bake in the oven for 30 minutes, until golden.

Puff Pie

PUF BOREK

There is a choice of fillings for this borek: *one is a meat-based mixture and the other uses feta cheese.*

Serves 6

300 g/10 oz plain flour
15 g/½ oz margarine
1 egg yolk
Salt
30 g/1 oz butter, melted
Olive oil, for shallow frying

FOR THE MEAT FILLING
175 g/6 oz minced beef or lamb
2 onions, finely chopped
Salt and ground black pepper

FOR THE CHEESE FILLING
15 g/½ oz margarine
250 g/8 oz feta cheese, mashed
1 egg white
60 g/2 oz chopped fresh parsley
Ground black pepper

PREPARATION TIME: **1 HOUR STANDING TIME PLUS 45 MINUTES**
COOKING TIME: **25 MINUTES**

1. Sieve the flour into a large bowl and knead with water, the egg yolk, margarine and a little salt, to a soft, workable dough. Cover with a wet tea towel and set aside for 1 hour.

2. Divide the dough into six equal pieces and roll each one out to an 20-cm/8-inch circle. Brush each circle with a little melted butter and place on top of each other. Cover with a damp tea towel again and allow to stand for 1 hour more.

3. To prepare the meat filling, melt the margarine and fry the meat with the onions. Season with salt and pepper. For the cheese filling, mix the cheese with egg white, parsley and pepper.

4. Roll a circle of dough as thin as possible. Place a spoonful of the filling on one half of the circle, then fold the other half over the top. Seal the edges with a little water. Repeat with the remaining circles.

5. Heat the oil in a large frying pan and fry the pastries evenly. Drain and serve hot.

Water Pie

SU BOREGI

This is a very light and delicious pie with a crispness to it which comes from immersing the pastry in water. You can serve it as an appetiser, or as a dessert if you change the filling to jelly, lemon cheese, or mincemeat, dusted with confectioners' sugar.

Serves 6

450 g/1 lb plain flour
3 eggs
1 Tbsp salt
75 g/3 oz cornflour
100 g/4 oz margarine

FOR THE FILLING

30 g/1 oz margarine
1 large onion, chopped
200 g/7 oz minced lamb
Salt and ground black pepper
1 Tbsp chopped fresh parsley

PREPARATION TIME: **1½ HOURS**
COOKING TIME: **1½ HOURS**

1. Sieve the flour into a bowl and make well in the centre. Break the eggs into the well and mix the flour with the eggs, gradually adding water and the salt. Knead to a soft dough, adding a little more water as necessary. Divide into nine pieces, one of them twice the size of the other eight. Flatten each piece and cover with damp tea towel. Allow to stand for 30 minutes.

2. Meanwhile, prepare the filling. Heat the margarine in a frying pan and fry the onions until transparent. Add the minced lamb and season. Cover and cook over medium heat. Finally, stir in the fresh parsley and allow to cool slightly before using.

3. You will need a 22-cm/9-inch round baking sheet. On a floured board, roll the largest piece of dough to twice the size of the baking sheet. Brush the baking sheet with a little margarine and line with the largest piece of dough. Roll the rest of the dough pieces into 22-cm/9-inch circles and place on top of each other, sprinkling cornflour between each layer.

4. Have ready a large bowl of cold water. In a large pan, bring 4½ litres/4¼ quarts water to a boil, with 1 tablespoon salt, and immerse each circle individually in the boiling water for 1 minute. Drain each layer, dip in the cold water, and drain again.

5. Preheat oven to 190ºC/375ºF/Gas Mark 5. Melt the margarine and place four of the circles on the baking sheet, brushing between each layer with the margarine. Spread the filling evenly and repeat the same process with the remaining four dough circles. Fold the edges of the larger one over and seal with melted margarine.

6. Bake for 1½ hours. Carefully invert the borek onto a serving dish and serve hot.

Talas Pie

TALAS BOREK

The talas ici, *the stuffing for the Talas Pie, is quite time-consuming to make, so ensure you have plenty of time in which to prepare this dish. Make the pastry while the filling is cooking as it needs to rest before being used.*

Serves 6

300 g/10 oz plain flour
15 g/½ oz margarine
2 Tbsp water
1 tsp salt
60 ml/2 fl oz olive oil
1 egg yolk

FOR THE STUFFING
30 g/1 oz margarine
2 onions, chopped
1 kg/2 lb lean lamb, diced
1 Tbsp tomato purée
1 tsp dried thyme
Salt and ground black pepper

PREPARATION TIME: **1 HOUR 40 MINUTES**
COOKING TIME: **1½ HOURS STANDING TIME PLUS 30 MINUTES**

1. For the stuffing, melt the margarine in a saucepan and fry half the onion and the meat, until the meat juices are reabsorbed. Stir in the tomato paste and add 250 ml/½ pt hot water. Bring to the boil and simmer for 1 hour. Add the remaining onion and simmer for 30 minutes more. Add the thyme and seasoning, mix well, and set aside until needed.

2. To make the pastry, sieve the flour into a large bowl, add the margarine, water and salt, and knead to a soft dough. Cover the dough with a wet tea towel and leave for 1 hour.

3. Roll out the dough to a 1-cm/½-inch thick rectangle. Cut the pastry into 12 equal pieces and allow to stand for 15 minutes.

4. Preheat oven to 190ºC/375ºF/Gas Mark 5. Now dip each piece of pastry in the olive oil and roll out as thin as possible. Place some meat filling in the centre of each one and fold the corners over to make packages.

5. Sprinkle an ovenproof dish or roasting dish with water. Beat the egg yolk with 1 teaspoon of the olive oil and 1 tablespoon water, then brush the pastries. Bake in the oven for 30 minutes, until evenly browned.

Shortbread
UN KURABIYESI

Cinnamon Cookies
TARCINLI KURABIYE

Raisin Cupcakes
UZUMLU KEK

Orange Cake
PORTAKALLI KEK

Chocolate Cake
CUKULATALI PASTA

Chocolate Mosaic Slices
MOZAYIK

Cookies and Cakes

BISKUVILER VE KEKLER

Shortbread

UN KURABIYESI

This shortbread is so simple to make. Children will enjoy helping you to shape the pieces and press in the almonds.

Makes 16

125 g/4 oz plain flour
125 g/4 oz butter
60 g/2 oz rice flour
4 Tbsp sugar plus extra for sprinkling
16 whole blanched almonds

PREPARATION TIME: **30 MINUTES**
COOKING TIME: **30 MINUTES**

1. Preheat oven to 170ºC/325ºF/Gas Mark 3 and butter a baking sheet. Blend the butter into the flour until the mixture resembles breadcrumbs. Add the rice flour and mix well. Stir in the sugar and knead to a smooth dough.

2. Break walnut-size pieces from the dough and flatten with your fingers, push an almond into the centre of each one, and place on the baking sheet.

3. Bake in the oven for 25 to 30 minutes, until pale brown in colour. Sprinkle with a little sugar. Transfer the shortbreads to a wire rack to cool and store in an airtight container.

Cinnamon Cookies

TARCINLI KURABIYE

Crisp and aromatic cookies—delicious at coffee time. They keep well stored in an airtight container.

Makes 20

100 g/4 oz margarine
100 g/4 oz sugar
225 g/8 oz wholemeal flour
1 egg
1 tsp ground cinnamon
20 whole blanched almonds

PREPARATION TIME: **30 MINUTES**
COOKING TIME: **25 MINUTES**

1. Preheat oven to 190ºC/375ºF/Gas Mark 5. Butter a baking sheet. Blend the margarine with the sugar until light. Beat the egg in a separate bowl with a little of the flour. Add to the margarine mixture, little by little, and, when mixed, stir in the flour and cinnamon. Knead the dough lightly until smooth.

2. Break off walnut-size pieces of dough, flatten with a fork dipped in hot water, and press an almond into each cookie.

3. Place on the baking sheet and bake in the oven for 25 minutes. Cool on a wire rack and store in an airtight container.

Cinnamon Cookies ▶

Raisin Cupcakes

UZUMLU KEK

This is a very easy cake mixture and gives good results every time. You can omit the raisins and use candied peel, glacé cherries, or a teaspoon of cocoa powder in their place. These cupcakes are baked in paper cups.

Makes about 15 cupcakes

100 g/4 oz margarine
100 g/4 oz sugar
2 eggs
100 g/4 oz self-raising flour
100 g/4 oz raisins

PREPARATION TIME: **10 MINUTES**
COOKING TIME: **25 MINUTES**

1. Preheat oven to 180ºC/350ºF/Gas Mark 4. Blend the margarine with the sugar until light. Beat the eggs in a separate bowl with a little of the flour. Then, little by little, add to the margarine mixture, stirring all the time. Stir in the flour, then the raisins, and mix well.

2. Place 2 teaspoons of the mixture in a paper cup. Repeat until all the mixture has been used up.

3. Bake the cupcakes in the oven for 20 to 25 minutes.

Orange Cake

PORTAKALLI KEK

The orange aroma is very intense and refreshing, and this lovely light tea-time cake is best eaten while fresh as it does not keep for long. Try serving it with a little whipped cream.

Makes a 450 g/1 lb loaf cake

100 g/4 oz margarine
100 g/4 oz sugar
1 Tbsp plain yoghurt
2 eggs
150 g/5 oz self-raising flour
1 tsp baking soda
1 tsp orange zest
1 Tbsp orange juice
Candied peel or orange slices, to decorate

PREPARATION TIME: **20 MINUTES**
COOKING TIME: **1 HOUR**

1. Preheat oven to 80ºC/180ºF/ Gas Mark very low and grease a 500-g/1-pound loaf tin. Blend the margarine and sugar together until light. Add the yoghurt.

2. Beat the eggs in a separate bowl with a little of the flour. Sift the rest of the flour with the baking soda and mix all the ingredients together.

3. Gradually add the eggs to the margarine mixture, stirring constantly. When mixed, add the flour. Finally add the orange zest.

4. Transfer the mixture to the loaf tin and bake in the oven for 1 hour. Transfer the cake to a wire rack and, while still hot, make a few skewer holes, and pour the orange juice over. Decorate with candied peel or orange slices.

Chocolate Cake

CUKULATALI PASTA

A cake for a special occasion. My chocolate cake is relatively easy to make with very good results, and the combination of pistachios and chocolate gives it a subtle, distinctive taste.

Makes a 20-centimetre/ 8-inch sandwich cake

170 g/6 oz margarine
170 g/6 oz sugar
3 eggs
200 g/7 oz self-raising flour
1 tsp baking powder
1 Tbsp cocoa powder
Zest of 1 orange
Chocolate vermicelli or chocolate curls, to decorate

FOR THE FILLING

150 g/5 oz butter, softened
1 Tbsp cocoa powder
250 g/8 oz icing sugar, sieved
1 Tbsp orange liqueur (optional)
30 g/1 oz pistachios, chopped (optional)

FOR THE FROSTING

90 g/3 oz icing sugar, sifted
30 g/1 oz cocoa powder
140 ml/¼ pt double cream

PREPARATION TIME: **1 HOUR**
COOKING TIME: **30 MINUTES**

1. Preheat oven to 190ºC/375ºF/ Gas Mark 5 and grease and line two 20-cm/8-inch round cake tins. Blend the margarine and sugar together until light. Add the eggs, one at a time, with a little flour. Beat thoroughly and stir in the cocoa powder and orange zest. Add the remaining flour and beat well.

2. Pour into the cake tins and bake in the oven for 25 to 30 minutes. Let the cakes cool slightly in the pans, then turn out onto a wire rack to cool completely.

3. To make the filling, combine the butter, cocoa powder, icing sugar, and orange liqueur, if using, together in a mixing bowl and beat well until smooth and glossy. Fold in the pistachios, if using. Sandwich the cakes together with the filling.

4. For the frosting, mix the sieved icing sugar with the cocoa powder in a mixing bowl. Stir in 2 tablespoons hot water and beat well until smooth. Spread evenly over the top with a knife dipped in hot water. Whip the double cream until thick then spread around the sides of the cake with a fork. Decorate with chocolate vermicelli or curls.

Chocolate Mosaic Slices

MOZAYIK

This is a children's birthday party favourite in Turkey. It is very easy to make and, as it is frozen, keeps well. I make it with petit beurre biscuits which you can get from any good supermarket.

Makes about 20 slices

500 g/1 lb petit beurre biscuits
100 g/4 oz butter or margarine
2 Tbsp cocoa powder
2 Tbsp sugar
4 eggs

PREPARATION TIME: **30 MINUTES PLUS 4 HOURS' FREEZING TIME**

1. Break the biscuits into crumbs by hand or with a rolling pin. Do not use a blender or food processor because you need small pieces, not powdered biscuits.

2. Melt the butter or margarine in a pan with the cocoa powder. When cooled, add 2 tablespoons water.

3. Place the sugar and the eggs in a blender or food processor and blend until smooth. Transfer to a bowl, stir in the cocoa mixture, and then the biscuit crumbs.

4. Place the mixture on a large piece of aluminium foil and roll it firmly into a cylinder shape. Freeze, wrapped in the foil, for 4 to 5 hours, then cut into slices, and serve. If you have some left over, wrap it in foil again and put it back in the freezer.

Tip

This recipe contains raw egg. Any woman who is, or suspects she is, pregnant should not eat it. Those with a weak immune system are also advised not to eat uncooked egg.

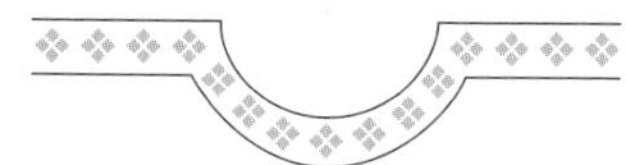

Desserts, Preserves and Drinks

TATLILAR

Baklava
BAKLAVA

Rice Pudding
SUTLAC

Flour Helva
UN HELVASI

Semolina Helva
IRMIK HELVASI

Fig Dessert
INCIR TATLISI

Piped Desserts
TULUMBA TATLISI

Pumpkin Dessert
KABAK TATLISI

Almond Dessert
SEKERPARE

Fruit and Nut Dessert
ASURE

Sweet Rice
ZERDE

Peaches with Raspberry Sauce
SEFTALI TATLISI

Chicken Breast Pudding
TUVUK GOGSU

Burnt Chicken Breast Pudding
KAZANDIBI

Fritter Balls
LOKMA

Turkish Delight
LOKUM

Rose Petal Preserve
GUL RECELI

Quince Preserve
AYVA RECELI

Yoghurt Drink
AYRAN

Sugar Syrup Drink
SHERBET

Turkish Coffee
KAHVE

Baklava

BAKLAVA

This is a simple-to-make version of the famous dessert. The baklava can be prepared using ready-made filo pastry—you will need 24 sheets—which reduces the preparation time considerably. However, I have given the ingredients for the dough if you would prefer to do it yourself. If you do, make sure you roll out the pastry sheets thinner than filo pastry.

Makes 24 pieces

FOR THE PASTRY

250 g/8 oz flour
2 eggs
1 tsp salt
1 Tbsp water
1 tsp olive oil
200 g/7 oz cornflour
175 g/6 oz unsalted butter, melted

FOR THE FILLING

175 g/6 oz unsalted butter
250 g/8 oz walnuts or pistachios, finely chopped
60 g/2 oz light brown sugar

FOR THE SYRUP

225 g/8 oz sugar
1 Tbsp lemon juice

PREPARATION TIME: **15 MINUTES**
COOKING TIME: **30 MINUTES**

1. For the pastry, sieve the flour and mix in the eggs, salt and 1 tablespoon water. Knead for 15 minutes, cover with a damp tea towel, and leave for 1 hour to rise.

2. Meanwhile, prepare the filling. Mix the chopped nuts with sugar and spread this evenly over the pastry. Melt the butter and drizzle over the filling.

3. When the pastry dough has been standing for 1 hour, spread the olive oil over the dough, knead again, and leave for 15 minutes more.

4. Cut the dough into eight equal pieces and sprinkle each with cornflour. Now roll each piece into a 15-cm/6-inch circle, sprinkle with cornstarch, and place on top of each other. Leave for 20 minutes. Then roll out the dough again, thinner than filo pastry, in rectangles. The layers of dough can be rolled out all together, but they should be alternated each time. Pile up the pastry sheets and cut them exactly the same size as your cake tin.

5. Preheat oven to 220ºC/425ºF/ Gas Mark 7. Brush a 18- by 22-cm/ 7- by 9-inch shallow cake tin with melted butter and place half the pastry sheets, brushing each one with butter, in the cake tin. Spread the filling evenly, then place the remaining sheets on top, brushing each with butter. Cut through all the layers of the pastry with a sharp knife to make six rectangles, then criss-cross each rectangle to create 24 triangular, bite-size shapes.

6. Bake in the oven for 15 minutes, then reduce the oven temperature to 180ºC/350°F/Gas Mark 4 and bake for a further 15 minutes until the pastry is crisp and golden.

7. Meanwhile, for the syrup, heat 250 ml/¼ pt water with the sugar and lemon juice in a saucepan. Bring to the boil and simmer for 15 minutes. Chill.

8. Remove the baklava from the oven and allow to cool in the pan. Pour the chilled syrup over the entire pastry. Allow to cool completely before recutting the shapes.

Rice Pudding

SUTLAC

This is one of the country's oldest recipes. It is very nutritious and a good dessert to serve to children. Although I like to serve it with jam, in Turkey it would always be served plain. This version, with a crust on top, is delicious.

Serves 4

1 Tbsp short-grain rice, washed
1 1/2 pts milk
1 Tbsp rice flour
1 tsp cornflour
250 g/8 oz sugar
Ground cinnamon, to decorate (optional)

PREPARATION TIME: **10 MINUTES**
COOKING TIME: **25 MINUTES**

1. Preheat oven to 190ºC/375ºF/Gas Mark 5. Cook the rice in water just to cover. Then heat the milk in a saucepan and add the rice. Bring to the boil and simmer.

2. Mix the rice flour and cornflour in a bowl with a little water to make a smooth paste, then pour this into the simmering milk, stirring constantly.

3. Add the sugar and stir until the mixture thickens. Divide among four individual ovenproof bowls, and bake in the oven until a light brown crust forms on the top. Sprinkle with cinnamon. Serve hot or cold.

Flour Helva

UN HELVASI

Prepare this traditional dessert beforehand and keep it in the refrigerator ready for a dinner party, but remember to serve it at room temperature.

Serves 6

250 g/9 oz margarine
500 g/1 lb plain flour
50 g/2 oz pine kernels
500 ml/½ pt milk
600 g/1¼ lb caster sugar

PREPARATION TIME: **30 MINUTES**

1. Melt the margarine and stir in the flour. Keep on stirring over medium heat until the flour is very light brown in colour. Add the pine kernels and, still stirring, brown them slightly.

2. Pour over 250 ml/¼ pt water. Boil the milk with the sugar in a separate pan and pour it into the helva mixture. Stir once, cover, and cook over medium heat until all the liquid is absorbed.

3. Stir again and, while still hot, take tablespoon-size pieces out, shape, and serve on individual plates.

◀ ***Flour Helva***

Semolina Helva

IRMIK HELVASI

This recipe, like the other helva dishes, dates back to the Ottomans, and is a formal dish usually only cooked on special occasions. It is very light in consistency and delicately flavoured by pine kernels.

Serves 6

250 g/9 oz butter
500 g/1 lb semolina
50 g/2 oz pine kernels
1 1/2 pts milk or half water, half milk
500 g/1 lb caster sugar
75 g/3 oz icing sugar

PREPARATION TIME: **10 MINUTES**
COOKING TIME: **30 MINUTES**

1. Melt the butter in a large saucepan, then add the semolina and pine kernels together, and cook until the pine kernels change colour, stirring continuously.

2. Bring the milk to the boil in a separate saucepan and stir in the caster sugar. Pour the milk over the semolina and pine kernels, stir once, cover, and cook for 3 minutes over high heat, 3 minutes over medium heat, and 3 minutes over low heat, until the milk is absorbed. Allow to stand over very low heat for 10 minutes.

3. Divide half the helva among six individual dishes and sprinkle with the icing sugar. Then, using a spoon, firm the remaining helva against the side of the pan and arrange it in the individual dishes on top of the other helva. Serve hot or cold.

Fig Dessert

INCIR TATLISI

This is an unusual and delicious dessert from the Aegean, where figs are plentiful. Although simple, it is quite filling.

Serves 4

500 g/1 lb dried figs
100 g/4 oz chopped mixed nuts
100 g/4 oz sugar
140 ml/¼ pt clotted cream, to serve

PREPARATION TIME: **20 MINUTES**
COOKING TIME: **20 MINUTES**

1. Preheat oven to 190ºC/375ºF/Gas Mark 5 and butter an ovenproof dish. Mix together the chopped nuts and sugar.

2. Cut off the stalks of the figs and, with your fingers, open up the central cavity. Fill each fig with the nut mixture. Place in the ovenproof dish with 250 ml/½ pt hot water. Cook in the oven for 20 minutes, basting occasionally. Allow to cool and serve with the cream.

Fig Dessert ▶

Piped Desserts

TULUMBA TATLISI

If you have a sweet tooth, then this is the recipe for you. It is a very traditional dessert, dating back to the Ottomans. I give the recipe here with less sugar than would normally be used in Turkey.

Serves 4

FOR THE SYRUP

500 g/1 lb sugar
Juice of ½ lemon

FOR THE PASTRY

100 g/4 oz butter
Pinch of salt
1 Tbsp sugar
250 g/9 oz flour
4 eggs
Olive oil, for shallow frying
50 g/2 oz shelled pistachios, chopped, to decorate

PREPARATION TIME: **20 MINUTES**
COOKING TIME: **1 HOUR**

1. For the syrup, place the sugar and lemon juice in a large saucepan, add 350 ml/¾ pt water, and bring to boil. Simmer for 15 minutes until thickened slightly. Allow to cool.

2. For the pastry, heat 350 ml/¾ pt water in a saucepan and add the butter, a pinch of salt and the sugar. Bring to the boil and, stirring rapidly, add the flour. Stirring continuously, simmer for 10 minutes, then turn off the heat, and allow to cool. When cool, knead with the

3. Put a little dough at a time into a piping bag fitted with a 1 cm/½ inch star or plain piping nozzle, and pipe 5 cm/2 inches lengths of pastry onto baking parchment.

4. Place the pastries in a frying pan with some olive oil. Heat the oil but do not stir. When the pastries harden on one side, turn them over and fry on the other side until golden. Drain, place in a serving dish, pour the cold syrup over the pastries, and sprinkle with the chopped pistachios.

Pumpkin Dessert

KABAK TATLISI

What do you do with the flesh of a Hallowe'en pumpkin? This is a good way to use those shapeless chunks. Scoop out the seeds and then cut the flesh into pieces. Arrange them in a serving dish and sprinkle with the nuts.

Serves 4

1 kg/2 lb pumpkin
300 g/10 oz sugar
150 g/5 oz shelled walnuts, chopped
Double cream, whipped

PREPARATION TIME: **30 MINUTES**
COOKING TIME: **40 MINUTES**

1. Seed and peel the pumpkin and cut into 12- by 7-cm/5- by 3-inch wide pieces. Arrange in a shallow dish half filled with water. Cook over medium heat until tender.

2. Add the sugar when the liquid is reduced, cover, and cook until the sugar is dissolved. Simmer without the lid until the syrup is thickened.

3. Remove from heat and place in a serving dish. Sprinkle with walnuts and serve cold with cream.

Pumpkin Dessert ▲

Almond Dessert

SEKERPARE

This is a good dessert after a big dinner. When served in individual dishes, it looks neat, pretty, and is delicately sweet.

Serves 4

1 egg
1 egg yolk
100 g/4 oz caster sugar
200 g/8 oz butter, softened
500 g/1 lb plain flour
A few drops of vanilla extract
About 16 whole blanched almonds

FOR THE SYRUP
250 g/8 oz sugar
Juice of ½ lemon

PREPARATION TIME: **20 MINUTES**
COOKING TIME: **45 MINUTES**

1. For the syrup, put the sugar and lemon juice into a saucepan with 250 ml/8 fl oz water, and bring to the boil. Simmer until the syrup thickens, turn off the heat, and allow to cool.

2. Beat the egg and egg yolk with the sugar and add the softened butter. Add the flour and vanilla extract, and mix well.

3. Preheat oven to 190ºC/375ºF/ Gas Mark 5 and butter an ovenproof dish. Take walnut-size pieces of dough and roll in the palms of your hands to make small balls. Press and flatten slightly. Arrange in the dish, leaving space between. Place an almond in the center of each one. Bake in the oven for 35 minutes, until nicely browned.

4. Pour the syrup over and leave the pastries to cool before placing in a serving dish.

Fruit and Nut Dessert

ASURE

This is one of my favourite desserts. It is rich and nutritious with nuts, figs, raisins and chick peas. I use pure wheat germ for this recipe which you can obtain from health-food shops. You can instead use any pure wheat cereal. The wheat will incorporate while cooking, but it requires a lot of water. It is a very famous dessert dating back to the Ottomans, when it was cooked in giant casseroles to celebrate the coming of spring.

Serves 6

450 g/1 lb natural wheat germ
100 g/4 oz kidney or haricot beans
250 g/9 oz chick peas
1 Tbsp raisins
450 g/1 lb caster sugar
100 g/4 oz shelled, skinned, and chopped hazelnuts
200 g/7 oz shelled, skinned, and chopped walnuts
4 dried figs, finely chopped
A few drops of rose oil, to sprinkle
Seeds of 1 pomegranate, to decorate

PREPARATION TIME: **20 MINUTES PLUS OVERNIGHT SOAKING TIME**
COOKING TIME: **5 HOURS**

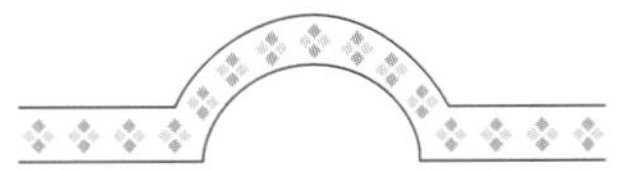

Tip

The cooking time for Fruit and Nut Dessert is five hours. To speed things up, you could use a pressure cooker. After soaking the wheat, beans and raisins overnight, place all the ingredients together in the cooker and cook for 30 minutes.

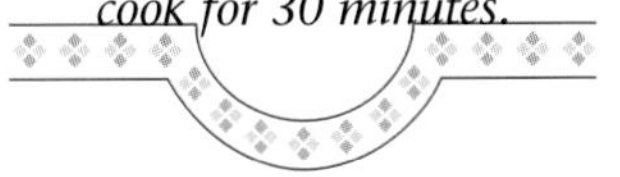

1. Soak the wheat, beans, chick peas and raisins overnight.

2. The next day, in a large saucepan, cook the wheat in plenty of water. Skim off the foam with a large spoon while boiling. Cover and cook over medium heat for 4 hours, until soft.

3. Cook the haricot beans and chick peas in water separately until soft, according to the package instructions.

4. When the water of the wheat thickens, add the sugar and drained chick peas and haricot beans. Cook for 1 hour more. Remove from the heat and stir in the hazelnuts, walnuts, raisins and figs.

5. Place in individual dishes and, when cooled, sprinkle with a little rose oil and decorate with pomegranate seeds.

Sweet Rice

ZERDE

The inclusion of saffron makes this such an attractive dish. Its colouring is exquisite and it makes a lovely end to any meal.

Serves 4

125 g/5 oz short-grain rice
100 g/4 oz sugar
A few saffron strands
1 Tbsp arrowroot
1 Tbsp currants
1 Tbsp chopped mixed nuts, to decorate
Seeds of 1 pomegranate, to decorate

PREPARATION TIME: **20 MINUTES**
COOKING TIME: **40 MINUTES**

1. Wash the rice and place in 1 l/2 pts water with the sugar. Bring to the boil and simmer for 20 minutes.

2. Soak the saffron in a little warm water, then add to the rice. Dissolve the arrowroot to a smooth paste in a little cold water, then add to the rice with the currants. Mix well and simmer over medium heat for 20 minutes until thickened.

3. Divide the mixture among individual bowls and leave to cool. Sprinkle with chopped nuts and pomegranate seeds, and serve.

Peaches with Raspberry Sauce

SEFTALI TATLISI

This is a wonderful dessert to serve when the fruit are in season. They make a refreshing combination for the end of a meal.

Serves 2

2 fresh peaches, washed
225 g/8 oz raspberries
60 g/2 oz sugar
Double cream, whipped

PREPARATION TIME: **5 MINUTES**
COOKING TIME: **20 MINUTES**

1. In a small saucepan bring 500 ml/1 pt water to the boil. Place the washed peaches in the water and lower the heat. Cook gently for 7 minutes, then drain, and peel the peaches. Chill for 2 hours.

2. Place the raspberries in a saucepan with the sugar, mix well, and bring to the boil. Take off the heat and push through a metal sieve to remove the seeds.

3. Place the peaches on a serving dish, with the raspberry sauce spooned over, and a little double cream or sour cream.

Sweet Rice ▶

Chicken Breast Pudding

TAVUK GOGSU

Although sounding strange to newcomers to Turkish cooking, this dessert is simply delicious and I have never known anyone who did not like it. The restaurants on the banks of the Bhosphorus in Istanbul feature it regularly on their menus. The taste is not reminiscent of the chicken at all, but its origins, and the idea of using chicken in a milk dessert, are lost in the mists of time.

Serves 4

Half a chicken breast
1 1/2 pts milk
250 g/9 oz sugar
Salt
1 Tbsp cornflour
150 g/5 oz ground rice
Ground cinnamon, for sprinkling

PREPARATION TIME: **20 MINUTES**
COOKING TIME: **50 MINUTES**

1. Cook the chicken breast in water until tender. Drain and cut crosswise into 5 cm/2-inch long pieces. Rub these pieces between the palms of your hands and tear into thin fibres. Soak the fibres in warm water then squeeze them to extract excess water. Repeat twice, changing the water each time.

2. Place the milk, sugar and some salt in a saucepan and bring to the boil, stirring continuously. Mix the cornflour and the ground rice with a little of the milk to a smooth paste. Stirring, pour the paste slowly into the milk and simmer until the milk starts to thicken.

3. Add the chicken fibres and reduce the heat. Simmer until thickened, stirring all the time. To check the consistency, pour a little of the mixture onto a plate. Allow to cool and turn the plate upside-down. It should come off completely without sticking to the plate.

4. Pour the mixture into a 3-cm/1-inch deep dish and allow to cool. Cut out four equal portions and roll each one into a cylinder shape. Sprinkle with cinnamon to serve.

Burnt Chicken Breast Pudding

KAZANDIBI

This is a classic of Ottoman cuisine and still very popular. It is served with ice cream in Istanbul and it is truly delicious.

Serves 4

Half a chicken breast
1 1/2 pts milk
250 g/9 oz sugar
Salt
1 Tbsp cornflour
150 g/5 oz ground rice
Ground cinnamon, for sprinkling

PREPARATION TIME: **50 MINUTES PLUS COOLING TIME**

1. Prepare the Chicken Breast Pudding (above) but pour the mixture into a heatproof, 3-cm/1-inch deep dish. Put the dish over a gas flame and brown the underside evenly, moving the dish over the flame if necessary.

2. Allow to cool for 2 hours, then cut it into four equal square pieces. Transfer to a serving dish and fold each piece like a thick roll. Place the browned side upward and sprinkle with cinnamon.

Burnt Chicken Breast Pudding ▶

Fritter Balls

LOKMA

These fried batter balls have syrup poured over before serving. If you prefer, you could dip them in honey.

Serves 4

FOR THE SYRUP

100 g/4 oz sugar
1 Tbsp lemon juice

FOR THE BATTER

200 g/7 oz plain flour
15 g/½ oz yeast
1 Tbsp butter, melted
Salt
Oil, for shallow frying
Ground cinnamon, for sprinkling

PREPARATION TIME: **30 MINUTES**
COOKING TIME: **1 HOUR PLUS STANDING TIME**

Tip

Cook these little dough balls in small batches to ensure the oil retains its heat and the balls quickly acquire a golden brown coating

1. For the syrup, put the sugar and lemon juice in a saucepan with 100 ml/4 fl oz water and bring to the boil. Simmer for 15 minutes then take off the heat.

2. Sieve the flour into a mixing bowl, then add the yeast, butter and a little salt. Mix well, then add 200 ml/7 fl oz water gradually while stirring. Make a soft dough and leave in a warm place for 1 hour.

3. Heat the oil in a frying pan. Take hazelnut-size pieces of the dough with a wet spoon and fry gently in batches of eight. Remove the balls as they are cooked and drain on kitchen towels.

4. Fry the balls for a second time until nicely browned, turning occasionally. Drain and pour the syrup over, covering the balls evenly. Then drain again and serve hot sprinkled with cinnamon.

Turkish Delight

LOKUM

I give the better-known rose-water version of these famous sweets, dating back to the fifteenth century. You can also make them with the addition of pistachios, almonds or coconut for a more traditional version.

Makes about 25

450 g/1 lb sugar
A pinch of cream of tartar or 25 g/1 oz gelatine, dissolved in water
75 g/3 oz cornflour
200 g/7 oz icing sugar plus extra for dusting
A few drops of rose water
50 g/2 oz honey
1 Tbsp pistachios, halved

PREPARATION TIME: **20 MINUTES**
COOKING TIME: **1½ HOURS**

1. Put the sugar in a saucepan with 100 ml/¼ pint water. Bring to the boil, stirring until the sugar is dissolved. Boil until the soft ball stage, about 116ºC/240°F. Drop a little of the syrup into a bowl of cold water; if it forms a ball then it has reached the required temperature.

2. Remove the pan from the heat, stir in the cream of tartar or the dissolved gelatine. Blend the cornflour and the icing sugar with 1½ l/3 pts water in another saucepan. Bring to the boil, stirring all the time, then simmer until thickened and clear.

3. Gradually beat the cream of tartar or gelatine mixture into the cornflour mixture. Bring to the boil, stirring frequently, for at least 30 minutes until transparent.

4. Remove from the heat and stir in the rose water and honey. Pour half of the mixture into a greased 15- by 15-cm/6- by 6-inch, deep, square cake tin. Scatter the nuts over. Pour the remaining half into the tin. Leave in a cool place overnight, or until set.

5. Turn the *lokum* out of the tin and cut into squares with a knife dipped in icing sugar. Dust with more sugar to coat the squares well.

Rose Petal Preserve

GUL RECELI

This preserve evokes the delicate scents of a summer's day. It is not brought to setting point, so disregard the usual tests. It tastes delicious with slightly toasted white bread spread with unsalted butter. If you would like a dark colour preserve, use dark red fragrant rose petals.

Makes 500 g/1 lb

250 g/8 oz fragrant pink rose petals
1 1/2 pt water
1 kg/2 lb sugar
Juice of 2 lemons

PREPARATION TIME: **5 MINUTES**
COOKING TIME: **35 MINUTES**

1. Place the rose petals and water in a preserving pan. Cover and bring to the boil. Simmer for 5 minutes then stir in the sugar.

2. Boil rapidly with the lid off for about 20 minutes, until the syrup thickens slightly. Add the lemon juice and bring to the boil once more.

3. Turn off the heat and allow it to cool.

4. Pour into sterilised jars.

Quince Preserve

AYVA RECELI

There is a delicate fragrance to be enjoyed while cooking this preserve, and the beautiful colour that graces the breakfast table makes preparing Ayva receli *worthwhile.*

Makes 500 g/1 lb

1 kg/2 lb yellow quinces
250 ml/½ pt water
1 kg/2½ lb sugar
Juice of 1 lemon

PREPARATION TIME: **10 MINUTES**
COOKING TIME: **35 MINUTES**

1. Wash and peel the quinces. Scoop the seeds out and slice thinly.

2. Place in a preserving pan with the water and bring to the boil. Simmer until soft, then stir in the sugar. Simmer until the sugar is dissolved.

3. Add the lemon juice and boil rapidly until set. You can check the set by placing a teaspoon of the preserve on a cold plate. Allow it to cool sufficiently to run a finger through it. If the mixture wrinkles, it is set, if not simmer for a few minutes more and repeat the test.

4. Remove from the heat, allow to cool a little and pour into sterilised jars. Leave to cool completely before sealing the jars.

Yoghurt Drink

AYRAN

This is a very simple and refreshing drink, generally served very cold with Doner Kebap, *sandwiches or burgers. It can be purchased ready mixed in bottles or cartons all over Turkey, and locals will flavour the drink by adding fresh fruit of their choice.*

Serves 4

500 ml/1 pt thick plain yoghurt
500 ml/1 pt cold water
a dash of salt

1. Place all the ingredients in a blender and whisk until frothy.

2. Divide the froth among four glasses, followed by the remainder of the drink.

Sugar Syrup Drink

SHERBET

Traditional sherbets are made from a special sherbet candy which is made from sun drying, moulding and pressing mulberries, sour cherries, or flowers such as orchids and roses. This sugar syrup is the base for a variety of sherbets.

Serves 1

SUGAR SYRUP
50 g/2 oz sugar
250 ml/½ pt water

SHERBET
50 ml/2 fl oz cherry juice
50 ml/2 fl oz red grape juice
50 ml/2 fl oz mulberry juice or exotic fruit juice
50 ml/2 fl oz grapefruit juice
25 ml/1 fl oz sugar syrup
Carbonated lemonade or soda water
A few sprigs of mint
A slice of lemon

1. To make the sugar syrup: Dissolve the sugar in water over a moderate heat. Bring to the boil and simmer for 5 minutes. Allow to cool and then pour into a sterilised container. Cover and store in the refrigerator.

2. To make the sherbet: Shake all the ingredients together with a little crushed ice. Pour into a long glass and top up with chilled soda water or lemonade.

Turkish Coffee

To make Turkish coffee correctly does require a long-handled pot called a 'cezve'. These are made in different sizes, depending on the number of people for whom you are making coffee. If a cezve is not available, try using a small pan which can be placed on the flame, preferably with a long handle to avoid getting burnt while the coffee is boiling. A well-made coffee must have froth on the surface, so do not use too large a pan. You will need to buy either Turkish coffee, which can be found in specialist coffee stores, or have your coffee beans toasted and ground to a fine powder. Serve the coffee in tiny cups, with Turkish Delight.

Serves 2

1 tsp caster sugar, optional
2 tsp Turkish coffee

1. Measure cold water, by using the coffee cups, into the cezve. Stir in the sugar and bring slowly to the boil over a low heat.

2. Add the coffee, stir well and heat until the froth forms on top. Just at the moment it may boil over, remove from the heat and divide the froth into the cups.

3. Return the cezve to the heat and bring to the boil again.

4. Pour the remaining coffee into the cups and serve hot.

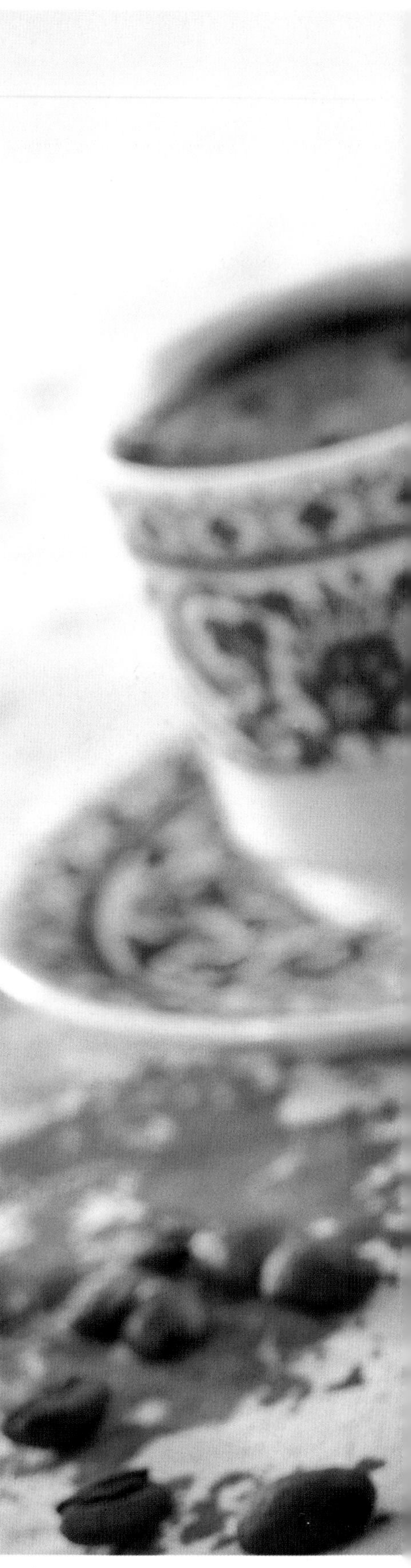